Peking Luck

Peking Luck

Roger Elliot

EASTERN UNIVERSITIES PRESS SDN. BHD.
Singapore   •   Kuala Lumpur   •   Hongkong

EASTERN UNIVERSITIES PRESS SDN. BHD.
112F, Block 5, Boon Keng Road, Singapore 12.
134 Jalan Kasah, Damansara Heights, Kuala Lumpur.
Stanhope House, 734 King's Road, Hong Kong.

Printed by Kok Wah Press (Pte) Ltd.

To Maggle The Horse

HOW TO USE THIS BOOK

There are five sections in my brand of Chinese astrology, called the Fivefold Path to Serene Understanding. These are: —

The Year — Twelve types of year in all, one of them refers to you. Descriptions of what each year means, and how you can find out which you are, are given in pages 19–73.

The Season — Five types of season in all, one of them indicates a part of your inner psyche. The meaning of each season, together with the way to discover which season you are, are given in pages 75–84.

The Fortnight — Twenty-four types of fortnight in all, one of them belongs to you. Read about the significance of your fortnight, plus the way to calculate which one you are, in pages 85–126.

The Day — Twenty-eight days in all, one of them tells you a lot about your emotional disposition. Details of each day, including the method of working out your own day, are given in pages 127–189.

The Hour — Twelve hours in all, one refers to your essential self. Read the details of the hours, plus the technique for working out your own hour, in pages 191–203.

If you wish, you can turn straight to these sections and quickly grasp the Chinese analysis of your character.

INTRODUCTION

This book seeks to unearth ancient Chinese astrology and present it in a clear modern light. It isn't a solemn academic treatise stuffed with learned quotations; neither is it a lightweight fun-book without any inner truth.

It's also a half-and-half book in another sense. It deals with Chinese astrology that's been rewritten by a Western astrologer to suit the way we live and think today. There's not a great deal here that a white-whiskered Mandarin would recognise as relevant to his own closed world. He was concerned with three main problems: long life, happiness and whether he would become a high government official. Today we are still interested in a healthy, pleasant life for ourselves and a few of us might even want to be civil servants; but beyond these simple objectives we have a wealth of opportunities and interests unknown to the Chinese of an earlier civilisation.

Partly this is due to the benefits of material progress. We travel more, we read more widely, we have a vast number of clever toys like rockets and computers to keep us preoccupied. But there are two other crucial reasons why the old Chinese methods of astrology need to be re-interpreted—and, at times, added to.

In the first place, we are far more interested in personal character than the Chinese—or any ancient peoples—were. We are fascinated by our own personalities, and the way they differ from those of our friends. Increasingly we view life as a process of self-fulfilment, of doing those activities that suit our individual temperaments. Other motives still exist: making money, being a success, leading an affectionate life with the right partner. But all of them are coloured by the overriding need to express our own unique character: to be ourselves. Success, long ago,

9

was living above the bread-line and getting preferment from the Emperor; everyone, from philosopher to paddy-worker, measured success in those terms. Today, each of us decides what we consider personal achievement to be. Your standards will be different from mine: not better, not worse, but different. And the difference is due to our recognition that you are a unique individual, as I am, and that we must follow our separate paths to happiness.

Hence the abiding modern interest in psychology, human nature and the way we get on with each other. Astrology, in ways that cannot be rivalled by other sciences, shares in this shift of emphasis away from 'What will happen to me?' towards 'Who am I?' In my everyday work as a consultant astrologer, I explain to clients that even if they have a burning single question about their future, it is better for them to understand why they need to ask the question in the first place—in other words, to understand who they are—instead of getting a pat answer and leaving my consulting-room none the wiser about their real needs as an individual.

This brings me to the second important reason why this book isn't 'pure' Chinese astrology. Just as we are far more interested in personality than mere fortune-telling, so do we have a much more intricate attitude towards the future than any of our ancestors did.

Take, first of all, our far greater range of opportunities and, just as significant, our greater social and economic mobility. A child growing up today has a vast number of career choices open to him. In the same way, this child can move up and down the social scale with total lack of embarrassment, if he so wishes. Indeed, the whole idea of class is becoming rapidly extinct.

Not so in Imperial China, say 2000 years ago. The emperor ruled over 50 million people whose rank was clearly established by an elaborate hierarchy of officials. There were 20 orders of rank bestowed by imperial edict. In addition, one's original family background, their wealth and social standing, all determined where on the ladder one was placed. Nobody could jump the queue; everything depended on gaining the favour of the bloke ahead, who might give a helping hand up.

Our attitude to the future is therefore wide-open and unlimited. Nothing, it seems, is impossible, provided we have the talent and energy to pursue it. But in the Han dynasty the avenues for advancement were few and strictly supervised, so that the opportunity to make progress might suddenly occur, out of nowhere, or might never turn up at all.

It's the same story in other fields: literally the agricultural fields of wheat, barley or rice. The farmer of those days had no reliable way of telling when the rains would come, and whether there would be a good or bad harvest, and whether a great famine would abruptly decimate the population. The Chinese lived in a black-and-white world, where Heaven suddenly shone with imperial or divine favour—or, equally without warning, darkened to produce disgrace or disaster.

Nowadays we crack jokes about the hopelessness of the weather forecasters to anticipate whether or not it will rain in the next few hours, but modern techniques, particularly the use of space satellites to forecast the direction of hurricanes, are gradually decreasing the area of uncertainty. And even if a prolonged drought occurs, a developed country has the resources to cope: plenty of reserve food supplies, marvellous new methods of soil husbandry, and the ability to plan ahead so that a single setback does not affect the overall production.

Planning is really the key to the difference between that old Chinese society and our own. They inhabited a world where blind chance seemed to raise them up or bitterly dash their hopes. No wonder, therefore, that they sought, through astrology and other forms of divination, to glean a morsel of hope for the future. No wonder, too, that so many of their fortune-telling techniques were essentially yes-and-no affairs, with no possibility for any inbetween alternatives.

Our own situation is almost totally removed from such a primitive world. It's true that occasionally a sudden twist of fate—illness, redundancy at work, a third world war—can reverse the pattern of our lives, but even these can be averted by preventive medicine, a sound economic policy and sensible diplomacy. By and large, however, we live in an ordered society where we create our own future through planning and foresight. Fortune-telling, in the old superstitious way, is quite out-of-date. We are in control of our own lives, not controlled by some mysterious alien destiny.

Modern astrology is concerned with the broad trends in life rather than absolute predictions. It isn't possible to know, with utter certainty, when a girl will marry, for instance; but it's easy enough for the experienced astrologer to say when she'll be liable to fall in love, or feel especially sexy. Astrology works from the inside out. It tells us what is happening in a person's heart, and only through inspired guesswork what is happening in the outside world.

These are the reasons why this book concentrates on your character rather than your destiny, and why the section on future trends deals with your moods and hopes and depressions instead of actual predictions of events. Man may not have complete free will, but he must behave as though he had. He must be responsible for his own future, and that means he must understand his own inner nature.

I hope this book helps you in your search for self-knowledge.

That said, I must explain that what appears in these pages must be treated with gentle scepticism. Some of it is culled from ancient Chinese sources, while other parts have been written in the light of western astrology. Oriental scholars may wince at some of the liberties I have taken, though I think they are justified.

For further reading about Chinese astrology, I suggest *The Origin of the Zodiac* by Rupert Gleadow (Cape) and *Science and Civilisation in China* by Joseph Needham (Cambridge University Press), especially vols. 2 and 3.

THE FIVEFOLD PATH TO SERENE UNDERSTANDING

Personal astrology, from whatever part of the world it originates, is based mainly on the positions of the heavenly bodies at the time of the individual's birth, and partly on their pattern in the sky at the time he wants a prediction about the future.

In the West, the main tools of the astrologer's trade are becoming well-known: the signs of the Zodiac, the planets themselves and the so-called aspects or angles between them. Many people know that a variety of astrological factors contribute towards a total understanding of the individual character. The most familiar of all is the Sun-sign, the segment of the Zodiac in which the Sun lay at the time of birth. From newspaper columns and articles in popular magazines, you would imagine that this Sun-sign described the whole of your personality and accounted for everything that might happen to you. But of course it refers only to one part of the character: the rock-bottom shape or framework on which the more transient of one's attributes seem to float. Equally important is the Moon-sign, where the Moon lay at birth. This describes one's emotional disposition, the kind of inner person one is, with all one's moods and secret fears and hopes. And thirdly there's the rising sign, the bit of the sky coming over the eastern horizon. This tells the astrologer about one's outer temperament, the superficial characteristics that one shows to the world but may not be true of one's inner thoughts and aims.

Now the Chinese had an equally wide variety of methods of discovering the truth about an individual's character and destiny. Leaving astrology aside, they developed some very complicated—and, to us, unlikely—techniques of divination. The oldest of all, and the weirdest, was scapulimancy, or the examination of oracle-bones. They were usually the shoulder blades of ox or deer, or maybe the shells of tortoises, which were heated with red-hot pokers. In these high temperatures the bones cracked; and it was the shape of these cracks, which way they wiggled and wriggled, that not only told the prehistoric Chinese whether there would be a good harvest or bad—but also led to the development of Chinese writing.

Another system consisted of drawing long and short stalks of dried corn, which had similarities to the best-known of all Chinese divination methods, the *I Ching*. Nearer astrology itself was chronomancy, a system of lucky and unlucky days based on the phases of the Moon that used to be included in all rural calendars before the Communists took over in China. And *thui ming*, or fate-calculation, was quite as elaborate as astrology, and surprisingly close in method. If a particular problem confronted you, the hour of the moment was added to the numbers corresponding to the day, month and year, and from the resulting equation could be gauged the answer to your troubles.

Chinese astrology itself based its predictions on the Moon, its distance above the horizon and closeness to planets and stars; the Sun, its position and colour; and the planets, especially when they rose above the horizon and formed conjunctions with themselves. To quote *Shih Chi*, written 2000 years ago: 'When Mercury appears in company with Venus to the east, and when both are red and shoot forth rays, then foreign kingdoms will be vanquished and the soldiers of China will be victorious.' Now the good news: 'When Mars follows Venus, the army will be alarmed and despondent. When Mars separates altogether from Venus, the army will retreat.'

The Fivefold Path

In this book I have selected five systems of Chinese astronomical calculation or astrological reckoning and brought them together to form a coherent way of understanding your own personality. This is known as the Five-fold Path to Serene Understanding.

Think of five woodland paths leading to a central glade, which is your own soul. Each path covers different terrain; indeed, you may not be able to see the other four paths from the one you are traversing. But having moved along all five paths you will have gained an overall knowledge of the whole surrounding landscape; and once you have gathered these paths at the point where they converge, you will have reached the stage of understanding the heart of your own nature.

The First Path

This deals with your underlying character, what motivates you to behave the way you do, and the direction in which your psyche is moving. It is based on your *year* of birth, according to the Buddhist, or Shaka, calendar. Broadly it corresponds with the Midheaven in western astrology, plus some Sun-sign characteristics.

The Second Path

This covers the vaguer territory of the path of under-foldment on which your soul is journeying. It cannot be translated easily into everyday terms, and its truth is more likely to be grasped by poetic intuition rather than strict logic. It is based on your *season* of birth, according to the ancient Chinese method of allotting one of five 'elements' to a particular time of year. It has no obvious correlation with western astrology.

The Third Path

This path, the closest to our western brand of astrology. deals largely with your whole approach to the community, particularly the kind of work you wish to tackle—and the sort of work you're likely to be skilled in. It is based on your *fortnight* of birth—or, more precisely, on which of 24 *chhi* (a period of 15·218 days) you were born. Clearly

17

this corresponds to the Sun-sign in western astrology, as far as it relates to career and political and social attitudes.

The Fourth Path

The fourth path describes your emotional disposition, the kind of inner consciousness in which you feel life rather than think about it. Obviously it deals largely with your ability to make friends and establish more intimate relationships. It is based on your *day* of birth, according to the position of the Moon in any of 28 *hsui* or ancient Chinese sky-segments. The link with western astrology is clearly with the Moon-sign.

The Fifth Path

The final path deals with that part of your psyche which is closest to the surface: the part that other people tend to notice at once, even though you may not always recognise the attributes yourself. It is based on your *hour* of birth, according to the old Chinese hour-circle of animals. This pathway is associated with the Ascendant, or rising sign, in western astrology.

Read the characteristics assigned to you in each of these methods of personality assessment, and then turn to page 204 where you will learn how to bring the paths together for total understanding.

THE FIRST PATH—Your Year of Birth

Introduction

Not so long ago, if you had asked a Peking rickshaw driver his age, he would have replied Dog, or Rat, or Cock. It is certainly a nosy question, especially from a Western visitor, but the Chinese would not have been making an appropriately rude reply. He would have been giving you a factual answer, for the Chinese man in the street, at least until the Communist revolution in 1949, used to signify a particular year by the name of an animal. It was far more interesting to them to know if you were a Rabbit person, say, than simply to be told you were born in 1939.

The reason is that each year is meant to possess certain characteristics, and the things that happen in that year, including the births of the new-born, all partake of the astrological influence of the animal concerned.

The Chinese gave each succeeding year the name of an animal. This habit may have begun as long ago as the sixth century B.C., and has been in evidence ever since. There are a dozen animals in all, so the cycle repeats itself every twelve years. The theory is that everybody born in a particular year shares certain qualities and motives. It's the same principle as the familiar Zodiacal signs used in Western astrology, only they refer to months instead of years.

It's daft to pretend that people born in any one year are all exactly the same. But maybe they do share something of the same outlook, just as kids at a school— though all individuals in their own right—share the same uniform.

More than that, the Tiger people of 1950 are meant to have something in common with the Tigers of 1938 and, before that, 1926; and, indeed, with the children being born in 1974, another Tiger year.

When you think about it, this does chime with reality. Often there can be a link between people a dozen years apart in age. They are separated by a curious in-between time-gap—shorter than the gulf between the generations, longer than the normal slight difference in age among friends. It's neither a parent-child relationship, nor a brother-sister one, but a genuine soul link, which is based on the Chinese animal years.

This ancient circle of animals has been applied to several different time systems. Originally it formed a twelve-fold division of the day into two-hour intervals, and it's this method which forms the basis of the Fifth Path starting on page 191. Sometimes, even today, it's used as an alternative to our own Zodiac. But it's hard to know which animal corresponds to which Sign. The Chinese themselves, when they think about it, correlate the Rat with Aries, the Ox with Taurus, and so on down the list. But this is a corruption of the original system, which may well have linked animals with the seasons when they were most active.

Gustave Schlegel, in his *Uranographie chinoise*, suggests that the Cock can be associated with October, because the cock in nature is a pretty angry creature, and in ancient China you always made preparations for war in October. It was the done thing.

Snakes ceased hibernating at the end of winter, Hares gave birth to their young in March and April, Tigers migrated in May, Rats were commonest in the hot days of July, and Boars were put out in August to trample and manure the water-logged ground.

Other writers such as Rupert Gleadow in *The Origin of the Zodiac* consider that the Snake corresponds to the October–November Sign of Scorpio, the Horse with the November–December Sign of Sagittarius (whose symbol is a Minotaur [half-man half-horse]) and the Sheep with the Christmas Sign of Capricorn the Goat.

My own conclusions, which are by no means dogmatic, are that the circle of animals, especially the Animal Years, are linked with our own Zodiac in the following fashion: —

RAT	A mixture of Libra and Aries
OX	Largely Taurus
TIGER	Leo, most of all
RABBIT	Cancer and Pisces
DRAGON	Nothing quite like it in the Zodiac, but a combination of Aquarius and Sagittarius seems closest.
SNAKE	Must be Scorpio
HORSE	Extrovert Capricorn, with a dash of Aries or Sagittarius
SHEEP	Capricorn and Virgo
MONKEY	Pure Gemini
COCK	Aries mostly
DOG	Partly Taurus, partly Virgo, even some Cancer
BOAR	No real comparison—bits of Aquarius, Virgo and Sagittarius.

What You Have To Do

Find out from the following Table what your animal year is. Read the characteristics given for that animal. Remember that these describe only a part of your overall personality: your underlying nature, the basic, rock-bottom kind of person you are even if your character doesn't appear like that on the surface.

Chinese years don't begin on the same day as ours do; their New Year's Day corresponds with the second New Moon after the winter solstice, which can vary between January 21st and February 19th.

TABLE OF ANIMAL YEARS
FROM 1880 TO 1980

10 Feb. 1880 — 29 Jan. 1881	DRAGON	see page 41
30 Jan. 1881 — 17 Feb. 1882	SNAKE	see page 45
18 Feb. 1882 — 7 Feb. 1883	HORSE	see page 49
8 Feb. 1883 — 28 Jan. 1884	SHEEP	see page 53
29 Jan. 1884 — 14 Feb. 1885	MONKEY	see page 57
15 Feb. 1885 — 7 Jan. 1886	COCK	see page 61
8 Jan. 1886 — 23 Jan. 1887	DOG	see page 65
24 Jan. 1887 — 11 Feb. 1888	BOAR	see page 69
12 Feb. 1888 — 30 Jan. 1889	RAT	see page 24
31 Jan. 1889 — 20 Jan. 1890	OX	see page 28
21 Jan. 1890 — 8 Feb. 1891	TIGER	see page 32
9 Feb. 1891 — 29 Jan. 1892	RABBIT	see page 37
30 Jan. 1892 — 16 Feb. 1893	DRAGON	see page 41
17 Feb. 1893 — 5 Feb. 1894	SNAKE	see page 45
6 Feb. 1894 — 25 Jan. 1895	HORSE	see page 49
26 Jan. 1895 — 13 Feb. 1896	SHEEP	see page 53
14 Feb. 1896 — 1 Feb. 1897	MONKEY	see page 57
2 Feb. 1897 — 21 Jan. 1898	COCK	see page 61
22 Jan. 1898 — 9 Feb. 1899	DOG	see page 65
10 Feb. 1899 — 30 Jan. 1900	BOAR	see page 69
31 Jan. 1900 — 18 Feb. 1901	RAT	see page 24
19 Feb. 1901 — 8 Feb. 1902	OX	see page 28
9 Feb. 1902 — 28 Jan. 1903	TIGER	see page 32
29 Jan. 1903 — 15 Feb. 1904	RABBIT	see page 37
16 Feb. 1904 — 3 Feb. 1905	DRAGON	see page 41
4 Feb. 1905 — 24 Jan. 1906	SNAKE	see page 45
25 Jan. 1906 — 12 Feb. 1907	HORSE	see page 49
13 Feb. 1907 — 1 Feb. 1908	SHEEP	see page 53
2 Feb. 1908 — 21 Jan. 1909	MONKEY	see page 57
22 Jan. 1909 — 9 Feb. 1910	COCK	see page 61
10 Feb. 1910 — 29 Jan. 1911	DOG	see page 65
30 Jan. 1911 — 17 Feb. 1912	BOAR	see page 69
18 Feb. 1912 — 5 Feb. 1913	RAT	see page 24

6 Feb. 1913 — 25 Jan. 1914	OX	see page 28
26 Jan. 1914 — 13 Feb. 1915	TIGER	see page 32
14 Feb. 1915 — 3 Feb. 1916	RABBIT	see page 37
4 Feb. 1916 — 22 Jan. 1917	DRAGON	see page 41
23 Jan. 1917 — 10 Feb. 1918	SNAKE	see page 45
11 Feb. 1918 — 31 Jan. 1919	HORSE	see page 49
1 Feb. 1919 — 20 Jan. 1920	SHEEP	see page 53
21 Jan. 1920 — 7 Feb. 1921	MONKEY	see page 57
8 Feb. 1921 — 6 Feb. 1922	COCK	see page 61
7 Feb. 1922 — 14 Feb. 1923	DOG	see page 65
15 Feb. 1923 — 4 Feb. 1924	BOAR	see page 69
5 Feb. 1924 — 24 Jan. 1925	RAT	see page 24
25 Jan. 1925 — 12 Feb. 1926	OX	see page 28
13 Feb. 1926 — 1 Feb. 1927	TIGER	see page 32
2 Feb. 1927 — 22 Jan. 1928	RABBIT	see page 37
23 Jan. 1928 — 9 Feb. 1929	DRAGON	see page 41
10 Feb. 1929 — 29 Jan. 1930	SNAKE	see page 45
30 Jan. 1930 — 17 Feb. 1931	HORSE	see page 49
18 Feb. 1931 — 6 Feb. 1932	SHEEP	see page 53
7 Feb. 1932 — 25 Jan. 1933	MONKEY	see page 57
26 Jan. 1933 — 13 Feb. 1934	COCK	see page 61
14 Feb. 1934 — 3 Feb. 1935	DOG	see page 65
4 Feb. 1935 — 23 Jan. 1936	BOAR	see page 69
24 Jan. 1936 — 10 Feb. 1937	RAT	see page 24
11 Feb. 1937 — 31 Jan. 1938	OX	see page 28
1 Feb. 1938 — 18 Feb. 1939	TIGER	see page 32
19 Feb. 1939 — 7 Feb. 1940	RABBIT	see page 37
8 Feb. 1940 — 26 Jan. 1941	DRAGON	see page 41
27 Jan. 1941 — 14 Feb. 1942	SNAKE	see page 45
15 Feb. 1942 — 4 Feb. 1943	HORSE	see page 49
5 Feb. 1943 — 25 Jan. 1944	SHEEP	see page 53
26 Jan. 1944 — 12 Feb. 1945	MONKEY	see page 57
13 Feb. 1945 — 1 Feb. 1946	COCK	see page 61
2 Feb. 1946 — 21 Jan. 1947	DOG	see page 65
22 Jan. 1947 — 9 Feb. 1948	BOAR	see page 69
10 Feb. 1948 — 28 Jan. 1949	RAT	see page 24
29 Jan. 1949 — 16 Feb. 1950	OX	see page 28
17 Feb. 1950 — 5 Feb. 1951	TIGER	see page 32

6 Feb. 1951 — 26 Jan. 1952	RABBIT	see page 37
27 Jan. 1952 — 13 Feb. 1953	DRAGON	see page 41
14 Feb. 1953 — 3 Feb. 1954	SNAKE	see page 45
4 Feb. 1954 — 23 Jan. 1955	HORSE	see page 49
24 Jan. 1955 — 11 Feb. 1956	SHEEP	see page 53
12 Feb. 1956 — 30 Jan. 1957	MONKEY	see page 57
31 Jan. 1957 — 18 Feb. 1958	COCK	see page 61
19 Feb. 1958 — 7 Feb. 1959	DOG	see page 65
8 Feb. 1959 — 27 Jan. 1960	BOAR	see page 69
28 Jan. 1960 — 14 Feb. 1961	RAT	see page 24
15 Feb. 1961 — 4 Feb. 1962	OX	see page 28
5 Feb. 1962 — 25 Jan. 1963	TIGER	see page 32
26 Jan. 1963 — 13 Feb. 1964	RABBIT	see page 37
14 Feb. 1964 — 1 Feb. 1965	DRAGON	see page 41
2 Feb. 1965 — 21 Jan. 1966	SNAKE	see page 45
22 Jan. 1966 — 8 Feb. 1967	HORSE	see page 49
9 Feb. 1967 — 29 Jan. 1968	SHEEP	see page 53
30 Jan. 1968 — 16 Feb. 1969	MONKEY	see page 57
17 Feb. 1969 — 5 Feb. 1970	COCK	see page 61
6 Feb. 1970 — 26 Jan. 1971	DOG	see page 65
27 Jan. 1971 — 18 Feb. 1972	BOAR	see page 69
19 Feb. 1972 — 2 Feb. 1973	RAT	see page 24
3 Feb. 1973 — 23 Jan. 1974	OX	see page 28
24 Jan. 1974 — 10 Feb. 1975	TIGER	see page 32
11 Feb. 1975 — 30 Jan. 1976	RABBIT	see page 37
31 Jan. 1976 — 17 Feb. 1977	DRAGON	see page 41
18 Feb. 1977 — 7 Feb. 1978	SNAKE	see page 45
8 Feb. 1978 — 27 Jan. 1979	HORSE	see page 49
28 Jan. 1979 — 15 Feb. 1980	SHEEP	see page 53

YEAR OF THE RAT

Dates

12 February 1888 — 30 January 1889
31 January 1900 — 18 February 1901
18 February 1912 — 5 February 1913
5 February 1924 — 24 January 1925

24 January 1936 — 10 February 1937
10 February 1948 — 28 January 1949
28 January 1960 — 14 February 1961
19 February 1972 — 2 February·1973

Your Basic Character

Your underlying motivation in life is the need to succeed without hurting anybody in the process. Getting to the top is important to you, but you want to do it in an elegant, artistic way.

Everyone born during a Year of the Rat has a bit more built-in taste than the majority of other human beings, but this doesn't turn him or her into a namby-pamby coward who runs away from the grim things in life. The Rat is beauty-plus-brawn, or style allied to strength.

You strive after perfection, taking a lot of trouble over niggly details, and you'll always finish a job once you've set your heart on it. The Rat Years are always characterised by a thoroughness in the way people behave — and those born at these times seem to possess extra stamina. Even when they fall ill, they fight back with wiry persistence to regain their good health.

The faults of you Rats are a tendency to be fooled by superficial appearances, or to pay too much attention to the decoration instead of the structure of anything. Sometimes you can be over-impressed by flashy intelligence, or a spot of genteel hypocrisy, or a show of class in egalitarian surroundings. What's more, you have a fatal tendency to tell white lies, even in circumstances when it's not necessary.

The Rat Child

The young Rat needs a good deal of molly-coddling — or rather, seems to want it, even though it may not be good for him or her. He's a relatively peaceful child until he mixes with other children all the time — then he retreats into a shell or overcompensates by often acting the bully. He's intelligent, attracted towards arts subjects if given the chance, and gradually becomes more firm-minded as he gets older.

The Extrovert Rat

You'll be either an extrovert or introvert (or a bit of both, but edging towards one or the other). As an extro-vert, you'll use your charm to get ahead in society, and may play one person off against another in order to achieve your ends. You'll find it easy to present a popular image to your fellow humans, but people may think differently about you once your back is turned.

The Introvert Rat

Here the fastidiousness is primarily directed towards artistic creation. You bring considerable delicacy of feel-ing to your friendships, but you don't make a great many acquaintances.

Rat Activities

Typical Rat sports are volley-ball, basket-ball, croquet and cricket—all of them calling for delicacy, power and seeming good manners, even though there's a lot of single-minded ambition underneath. There are also team games, at which Rats excel.

Rat hobbies are painting, interior decoration, crafts (including raffia-work), making soft toys and weaving.

It's very hard to generalise about Rat careers, but most Rats are good at dealing with other people and, if they're extrovert, like to project their personalities in a pleasing fashion. They like to feel they are spreading a little hap-piness and making the world a gayer, sweeter place in which to live.

What Goes with Rats

Countries believed to be associated with the Years of the Rat are South Africa, China, Japan, Tibet and the Balkan countries involving Greece, Turkey, Albania,

Yugoslavia and Bulgaria. It's possible the Congo is also linked to the Rat.

The various gems and semi-precious stones said to be connected with Rat Years are amethyst, diamond, garnet, bloodstone, jasper and malachite.

The following inventions were all made during Rat years: — Cellophane, stainless steel, long-playing records and transistors. There seems a strong link, too, with nuclear physics; the quantum theory, X-ray crystallography, gamma rays and the separation of uranium are all linked with Rat years.

Well-Known Rats

Typical Rat politicians are Richard Nixon and Enoch Powell, both combining power mania with a desire to present a charming image to their electorate. These are two introvert Rats, of course. Two Rat actors demonstrating grace and determination are Fred Astaire and Doris Day; an introvert Rat still displaying astonishing delicacy in his acting technique is Marlon Brando.

The American composer Aaron Copland and dramatist Tennessee Williams are also Rats; so is the British scriptwriter Robert Bolt. Perhaps the finest expression of the Rat character in this century can be seen in Lord Louis Mountbatten; he is self-evidently a man of principle who wears his authority with great charm and self-effacement.

Getting on with Others

Here's how the Rat people tend to harmonise—or conflict— with other Years: —

With other Rats: Quite well, but can sometimes seem like rival brothers or sisters: e.g. Charlton Heston and Marlon Brando.

With Oxen: Fine in amiable surroundings, but their obstinacy can seem like pig-headedness to you, and sometimes they seem dull.

With Tigers: Can be a clash of temperament, particularly concerning leadership. You like their warmth, not their wrath.

With Rabbits: Broadly a good link between you, but sometimes they seem too goody-goody to you. They want to stay home too often.

With Dragons: A very good relationship, especially at a mental level. It's a light, pleasant sort of compatibility.

With Snakes: A bit too intense for you, and sometimes too crude. If you find a subject in common, you can be great pals.

With Horses: Rather a love-hate relationship here, but never with much malice! Horses seem too boisterous, too ambitious.

With Sheep: A lot in common between you, but perhaps a lack of drive forcing you into each other's company.

With Monkeys: Perhaps your most compatible Year, for you can quickly establish a frothy, theatrical link warming all hearts.

With Cocks: Some sympathy between kindred spirits, but they tend to eat you up—with passion, anger or ruthless ambition.

With Dogs: They tend to be a bit boring, but you find stability with them, so it could be a placid, faithful relationship.

With Boars: Lovely for friendship, not good for grand passion. You can work well together, and enjoy each other's mental company.

YEAR OF THE OX

Dates

> 31 January 1889 — 20 January 1890
> 19 February 1901 — 8 February 1902
> 6 February 1913 — 25 January 1914
> 25 January 1925 — 12 February 1926

11 February 1937 — 31 January 1938
29 January 1949 — 16 February 1950
15 February 1961 — 4 February 1962
3 February 1973 — 23 January 1974

Your Basic Character

What makes you tick is your need for security—financial, emotional, any kind of security you can think of. You worry about loneliness, poverty, homelessness, and you feel happiest with a few pension plans in your pocket and a nice stable marriage partner by your side.

Provided you have these necessities, you're a marvellously solid, trustworthy individual: a creature of old-fashioned mahogany virtues who gets more set in your ways as the years pass. The creature comforts—food, drink, lovemaking, a nice armchair—mean a lot to you, and the older you get, the more you'll want to stay in the same old groove.

Nearly all Ox people have a deep urge towards creativity. Sometimes it takes the form of building up a business or running a fruitful marriage, sometimes it results in genuine works of art—paintings, books, theatrical performances in particular. You pay good attention to detail, though once you've decided what you're good at, you tend to stay in that routine, leading to certain familiar mannerisms.

Your faults are sluggishness, which can lead to a chronic health condition in some Oxen, and a selfish, acquisitive urge that should be curbed. You are decidedly social, but have inner resources of character that would enable you to survive on a desert island.

The Ox Child

The young Ox is a sturdy, self-sufficient child who starts early to establish independence from his parents. He's a placid infant if left to himself, a friendly character provided he's not pushed around too much. As a schoolchild he combines a strong interest in practical subjects with a liking for music, drama and painting. Broadly tolerant by nature, he'll suddenly throw a tantrum if really provoked.

The Extrovert Ox

You'll be either an extrovert or introvert (or a bit of both, but edging towards one or the other). As an extrovert, you'll be marvellously sociable, the life and soul of a party, very hail-fellow-well-met. People will find you generous, even extravagant, but watch your tendency to bully with good humour.

The Introvert Ox

You've a profound capacity to think deeply about the fundamental questions in life, but by retiring into yourself you can get an inferiority complex about yourself which is quite unjustified.

Ox Activities

Typical Ox sports are football (rugby and soccer), cross-country running, pot-holing and weight-putting. The Ox people get a big thrill from sheer bodily exertion over a long period of time.

Ox hobbies are painting and sculpture, do-it-yourself work, car maintenance and stock market dabbling. Gardening is a recurring joy for many Ox folk.

All remarks about Ox careers must be generalisations, but you work best in a job where care, prudence and steadiness are required. You like working with others, but once your mind is made up, you find it difficult to be flexible in your thinking. Artistic and financial occupations are broadly suitable.

What Goes with Oxen

Countries believed to be associated with the Years of the Ox are Eire, Cyprus, Palestine, Syria and Jordan. The Argentine in South America, Nigeria in Africa, and New

Zealand in Australasia are other probable Ox countries; Venezuela may also be included.

The various gems and semi-precious stones said to be connected with Ox years are moss-agate, emerald, coral, jade, alabaster and lapis lazuli.

The following biological/chemical discoveries and developments were made in Ox years: — the manufacture of adrenalin, the discovery of chlorophyll, the isolation of Vitamins A, B and B_2. Nylon stockings, jet engines and motor cycles are all linked with the Ox.

Well-Known Oxen

Two German politicians typify the best and worst of the Ox character: the goody is Willy Brandt, the baddy Adolf Hitler. Both displayed qualities of stubbornness, but in very different ways.

Creative Oxen have been Walt Disney, Vincent Van Gogh, Auguste Renoir, Charles Chaplin and, more recently, the English painter David Hockney.

In the acting profession, Peter Sellers and Richard Burton are both from the Ox Years—so is Tony Curtis. All, interestingly enough, have a stocky appearance, especially around the neck—a typical physiological trait among Oxen.

Perhaps the most quintessential Ox writer was Rudyard Kipling, who displayed all the robust humour, patriotism, belief in the common man, and strength of character associated with the Ox Years.

Getting On With Others

Here's how the Ox people tend to harmonise—or conflict— with other Years: —

With other Oxen: A good solid relationship, with the capacity to enjoy a good laugh together.

With Rats: Affable, but their quickness can nonplus at times, and their ability to swim with the tide lacks principle.

With Tigers: They can burn you up with anger, excitement, resentment, yet you cannot resist the magnetism of their appeal.

With Rabbits: Excellent links, especially for a placid family relationship. In business partnership you lack drive together.

With Dragons: You're intrigued by their mental gymnastics, but if there's a clash of wills, who's the one to give way? Nobody!

With Snakes: Real compatibility here, especially between husband and wife. You respect each other's power, respond to each other's presence.

With Horses: Good for practical affairs together, but a certain lack of emotional sympathy at times. Fine drinking pals!

With Sheep: Can prove a real love-hate match! Something in the Sheep character appeals—yet something else offends!

With Monkeys: They're too clever by half, and their approach to the world is more slapdash and easy-going than your own.

With Cocks: Excellent links here, especially for lovers. The steadiness plus richness of your character welds with Cock traits.

With Dogs: If you both dig in your heels, you get nowhere but glowering at each other. You can really be good friends if you try.

With Boars: Promising links, because you have a lot in common. The difficulty comes in being sensitive to each other's foibles.

YEAR OF THE TIGER

Dates

21 January 1890 — 8 February 1891
9 February 1902 — 28 January 1903
26 January 1914 — 13 February 1915
13 February 1926 — 1 February 1927

1 February 1938 — 18 February 1939
17 February 1950 — 5 February 1951
5 February 1962 — 25 January 1963
24 January 1974 — 10 February 1975

Your Basic Character

The drive in your life is the need to express your own self-esteem. This sounds nasty, and at times your vanity can drive the rest of us to distraction; but you also have warmth and sensuality, and magnetism of personality, to assemble a circle of admirers around you.

Without these faithful followers, you are liable to turn cynical and unhappy, but as long as one person is worshipping you (and there's always yourself!) life is worth living.

Other fine qualities you possess in good measure are courage, forthrightness and the desire to accept a risk in a good cause.

No Tiger person necessarily is spoiling for a fight, but if a challenge is issued, you feel your honour is at stake . . . and accept it you must. This is probably a fault, though a lovable one; this sense of the rightness of certain attitudes, even though they fly in the face of reason. The old-fashioned virtues of honour, chivalry and courtesy over and above the call of politeness can be included here.

Your faults, apart from those already mentioned, are a tendency to play with other people's emotions like a cat toying with a captured bird and an occasional blind spot as far as the notion of *compromise* is concerned: you don't know the meaning of the word. You like to be boss of any team, be it at work, on the playing field, or in your private affairs. And yet there's a terribly touching innocence about you—like the boy prefect, or the brave young officer thinking of war as a Noble Venture.

The Tiger Child

The young Tiger has a gaiety that is immensely engaging; but soon enough he feels the need for a victim to sharpen his claws on. He can throw tantrums if he can't get his own way, and needs a good example from his father—or father figures—if he's to learn how to hold authority as an adult. He should be sporty, friendly and not passionately keen on academic subjects—though arts like drama and painting should appeal.

The Extrovert Tiger

You'll be either an extrovert or introvert (or a bit of both, but edging towards one or the other). As an extrovert, you'll be very conscious of your need of an audience to clap you. The applause can turn your head, just as an over-narcissistic attitude can make you seem pompous and conceited to others.

The Introvert Tiger

You suffer from lack of confidence in getting your warmth across, so you may have delusions of grandeur quite out of keeping with your normal everyday personality.

Tiger Activities

Typical Tiger sports are motor racing, polo and horse racing, pole-vaulting, sprinting and real tennis. It's hard. for you to play a subordinate role in team games—you always want to grab the headlines.

Tiger hobbies are sun-bathing, metalwork (especially bronze casting), amateur dramatics, playing brass instruments (especially the trumpet) and dressing up.

The qualities the Tiger Year people bring to their careers are, first and foremost, the desire to take charge of the situation and seem to run the outfit. They like being admired for their personal attributes rather than their capacity for hard work. They can be terribly attractive individuals, but they can sometimes give way under pressure.

What Goes With Tigers

Countries believed to be associated with the Years of the Tiger are Italy and France, Chile and Ecuador, Uganda and the former territory of Bechuanaland, now Botswana. It's noticeable that major international crises occur during Tiger Years: the start of the First World War, the British General Strike, The Munich crisis preceding the Second World War, the start of the Korean War, and the Cuban missile crisis. The next Tiger Year is 1974!

The various gems and semi-precious stones said to be connected with Tiger Years are ruby, diamond, hyacinth, carbuncle and cat's-eye.

Two important inventions made during Tiger Years admirably sum up the potential violence and show-biz glamour of the Tiger character: dynamite and television.

Well-Known Tigers

Two international statesmen, born in the same year, illustrate the difference between the extrovert and introvert Tiger traits: Dwight D. Eisenhower, the sunny friend of all mankind, and Charles de Gaulle, megalomaniac man of destiny.

Tigers always need to operate on the grand scale—witness the great British engineer Isambard Kingdom Brunel (even the name is Tigerish!), the extravagant poetess Elizabeth Barrett Browning and two men of vision, their eyes fixed on the future: Karl Marx and H. G. Wells.

Tigers love to rule—with kindly authority. Queen Elizabeth II and her daughter Princess Anne are both graceful, bonny but dignified Tigresses of Royal blood.

Getting on With Others

Here's how the Tiger people tend to harmonise—or conflict—with other Years: —

With other Tigers: Like two monarchs—at best, united

against the world; at worst, always trying to score points off each other.

With Rats: Can be a clash of temperament, as you try to get your own way by forceful charm, the Rats by charm and guile.

With Oxen: You enjoy showing off in front of them, but in the last resort you either despise them . . . or secretly envy them.

With Rabbits: Nothing much in common, but that's why you're attracted to each other. You find them restful and motherly.

With Dragons: You operate on different wavelengths, but you can still work well in concert. You respect the other's will.

With Snakes: A terrific battle at times, with lots of arguments and far too much pride—but still friendship is possible.

With Horses: Plenty in common, with just enough difference to whet your appetite. Horses are your most compatible animal.

With Sheep: Not too much magic between you, though an adequate working relationship can be established. Good second-in-commands for you.

With Monkeys: You can't help being drawn towards their lively manners, even though there's always a note of comedy in their approach to you.

With Cocks: Lots of competition, but this can provoke admiration, not hatred. Together you can be too much of a good thing.

With Dogs: Of course you want to assume leadership, but if you give yourself time to learn, you can gain much wisdom from the Dogs.

With Boars: Not very many obvious links, meaning you can come together for a particular project but may get bored in the long run.

YEAR OF THE RABBIT

Dates

> 9 February 1891—29 January 1892
> 29 January 1903—15 February 1904
> 14 February 1915— 3 February 1916
> 2 February 1927—22 January 1928
> 19 February 1939— 7 February 1940
> 6 February 1951—26 January 1952
> 26 January 1963—13 February 1964
> 11 February 1975—30 January 1976

Your Basic Character

Your great talent is as nourisher and protector of those around you. You like to mother life, help it to grow— so that you are excellent at gardening, home-making, cooking, caring for sick or unhappy people, pouring out your heart to anyone willing to listen.

Even the male Rabbits display something of these womanly qualities; many of them have a soft centre, however bold and brave they seem in their outer temperaments. They have a sentimental streak, or a deep love of Nature, or a liking for women's company that is certainly not sissy.

Sometimes the softness emerges as artistic talent, though not a very revolutionary kind. The Rabbit writer has a deep sense of nostalgia for the past, just as many ordinary Rabbits have a kind of built-in emotional conservatism that grows stronger as they get older. Rabbits do not welcome change; they prefer the past, even if it's a bit tatty and faded!

As a Rabbit, you'll find it relatively easy to establish quick links with your kind of people and thus develop marvellous lasting relationships; but you are callous, at worst, towards people who aren't part of your family circle. This clannishness means you prefer the old familiar circle of cronies to the wider set of acquaintances.

Your faults are a tendency to take things too personally, to allow your imagination to get out of hand, to be too possessive of loved ones. There's usually a strong family feeling by Rabbits, with all the feuds and bitterness that families can produce.

You can also be more moody than other Years. At best, you always have a ready shoulder for people to cry on; at worst, you are a bit of a shrew, a complainer, a fusspot, a fuddy-duddy.

Your eventual aim in life is to find peace amid the turmoil of your own heart.

The Rabbit Child

The young Rabbit responds above all to the influence of his or her mother. Boys in particular often have special relationships, for better or worse, with the mother figure, and this can be awkward in adult life when the man must become self-sufficient. All Rabbit children develop a protective facade that may be different from their real inner sensitive selves. Parents should expect some guile, deception and sheer imagination to be at work in the young Rabbit's mind.

The Extrovert Rabbit

You'll be either an extrovert or introvert (or a bit of both, but edging towards one or the other). As an extrovert, you're polished but subtle in your dealings with others, able to be sincere without being embarrassed. You'll have mastered your own emotional nature, and want to display it to others in a vivid, dramatic way.

The Introvert Rabbit

Rabbits tend towards introversion. You'll be shyer than you want to be, more mixed-up in understanding your own feelings, making fewer friends but expecting a great deal from them.

Rabbit Activities

Typical Rabbit sports are hockey, wrestling, golf, rowing and cycling.

Rabbit hobbies are, for both sexes, the home-making skills; repairing broken objects, wood carving, upholstery, family games, social activities in homely neighbourhood clubs.

The qualities Rabbit people bring to their careers are a strong sense of service to the community (or, more selfishly, a desire for the family firm to prosper), an ability, by and large, to deal with other people and work for their welfare and happiness, and leadership so long as those under you are prepared to cooperate. You are much better in a crisis than you—and other people—expect.

What Goes With Rabbits

Countries believed to be associated with the Years of the Rabbit are Wales, Belgium and Holland, Switzerland, Canada and possibly Singapore. The Rabbit Years have often emphasised the role of women in public life, the advance in women's rights, and the development of child welfare, house building and international 'togetherness'—such as the *Entente Cordiale* between Britain and France.

The various gems and semi-precious stones said to be connected with Rabbit Years are emerald, black onyx, selenite, pearl especially, and crystal.

Well-Known Rabbits

Two national leaders exemplify similar—yet so different!—expressions of the Rabbit character. Ruling over the emerging British Empire was Queen Victoria, 'mother' to a quarter of the world's population. Fifty years later, as ruler over the emerging Soviet empire, was Joseph Stalin, the 'little father' of the huge Russian citizenry.

Many Rabbit authors have made names for themselves,

and nearly all of them demonstrate the Rabbit interest in family life or, on the wider scale, the quality of national character. None of them is particularly inventive, all of them are romantic conservatives: Walt Whitman, Henry Longfellow, John Galsworthy, E. M. Forster, Evelyn Waugh and Arthur Miller.

Two film actors—Cary Grant and Richard Benjamin —both demonstrate the softness and puzzlement of Rabbit folk. And David Frost beautifully illustrates the tough-tender, hard-hitting yet sentimental dichotomy of the Rabbit psyche.

Getting On with Others

Here's how the Rabbit people tend to harmonise—or conflict—with other Years: —

With other Rabbits: Excellently, as far as cosy friendships are concerned, but a bit too touchy for real driving business links.

With Rats: A good link, but they can be too devious at times for you, and their lack of principle can upset your morals.

With Oxen: Again good links, especially for placid family relationships. On emotional issues you can both be tenacious—for or against each other!

With Tigers: You're attracted by their verve and positive attributes. They like your peace of mind. Different, but quite good together.

With Dragons: Their appetite for power worries you, your real sense of sympathy touches them (and makes them guilty?).

With Snakes: Terrific magnetism between you, but it can turn to hatred unless the emotions are controlled.

With Horses: Quite a number of similarities, but there are bound to be some cross words, as they are more 'male' than you.

With Sheep: Plenty of compatibility here, but you aren't very brave together, nor energetic. A slight danger of niggly fussiness.

With Monkeys: Very different approaches to the world, so little in common. You can look after them, they can cheer you up.

With Cocks: Your opposite, for better or worse. You learn more from Cocks than any other animal, but the lesson may include pain.

With Dogs: A plodding, amiable sort of relationship, but they can occasionally snap at you, while you can retreat into sulks.

With Boars: Lots of togetherness, and you can easily spend the rest of your lives together. But you may not be adventurous enough as a couple.

YEAR OF THE DRAGON

Dates

> 10 February 1880 — 29 January 1881
> 30 January 1892 — 16 February 1893
> 16 February 1904 — 3 February 1905
> 4 February 1916 — 22 January 1917
> 23 January 1928 — 9 February 1929
> 8 February 1940 — 26 January 1941
> 27 January 1952 — 13 February 1953
> 14 February 1964 — 1 February 1965
> 31 January 1976 — 17 February 1977

Your Basic Character

Your purpose in life is a good deal more complex than that of people of the other animal years. You want power but will only use subtle, original ways to obtain it — with the results that your efforts can sometimes be self-defeating.

The Dragon Years have an added gloss of magic, inventiveness, resourcefulness about them, and you, by being born in one of them, share a little of this ingenious quality. There's something of the wizard about you: a person of some mystery to even your friends . . . not to mention yourself! You have a fine respect for reason and logic yet are happy enough to bypass them with a sudden hunch of your own.

You cannot help being attracted to the great mysteries of why we are here, where we are going, and how life works at all. The Dragon mind is alert, probing, full of concentration yet agile enough to leap to a new train of thought altogether.

You are capable of splendid affection but always remain a little distant, as though you never know when you might pack your bags and leave. Mental companionship means a lot to you, and there's often a stylish wit to your conversation—even, for some of you, a downright zany humour.

You are not particularly loyal, changing your mind overnight if your daemon tells you to, but you have marvellous courage if really forced out on a limb. Your other faults are a devious delight in bizarre events/ideas/people simply because there's a shocking quality about them; and a tendency to arouse the suspicion of others simply through deviousness over the years.

The Dragon Child

The young Dragon gets into a lot of mischief, and can be a nuisance simply because he or she is always asking 'why?' He needs establish his independence and will soon rebel against an over-restrictive parent. Special attention should be paid to his education—if necessary, with extra tuition or plenty of oddball extra-curricular subjects.

The Extrovert Dragon

You'll be either an extrovert or introvert (or a bit of both, but edging towards one or the other). As an extrovert, you'll be mentally flamboyant, given to flourishes of wit and epigram, keen to impress the other sex with your cleverness and charm. You'll enjoy practical work using your mind, such as engineering, computer studies and psychoanalysis.

The Introvert Dragon

You'll be the profound thinker, putting things down on paper rather than into your mouth. You'll still be rather friendly towards others, but you'll pick and choose your allies.

Dragon Activities

Typical Dragon sports are medium-distance running, show-jumping, ice-hockey and speedway racing. You aren't really an ideal member of a team, preferring a more individualistic role.

Dragon hobbies are electronics (including radio hams), debating, archaeology and oddball subjects like astrology and magic. In an orchestra the Dragon is drawn to electronic instruments, tympani and perhaps a harpsichord.

The qualities the Dragon Year people bring to their careers are inventiveness, a radical outlook and the ability to think on your own without the help of others. You can be a member of a team on a voluntary basis; but nobody, not even the most brilliant leader in the world, can coerce you into action against your will.

What Goes With Dragons

Countries believed to be associated with the Years of the Dragon are Spain, Ceylon, Cuba, Nepal, Finland, Bolivia and Kenya. There's always a note of radicalism in Dragon years, especially to do with the spread of popular democracy—so that the famous British Reform Bill, and the civil rights movement in the United States, are both Dragon events.

The next Dragon year, in 1976, should produce quite a few scientific advances, especially a new form of energy.

The various gems and semi-precious stones said to be connected with Dragon Years are sapphire, opal, chalcedony and amber. Synthetic stones can also be included.

Limelight, throwing a bright, eerie light on bigger-than-life dramatic events, was discovered in a Dragon Year. That sums up the Dragon contribution.

Well-Known Dragons

Two great 19th-century figures, born on the same day in the same year, revolutionised their particular fields of science and politics: Abraham Lincoln and Charles Darwin. Another politician, nearer our own day, is the subtle Soviet Prime Minister Alexei Kosygin. Another Head of State, who survived many vicissitudes in African politics, has been the Ethiopan Haile Selassie.

Typical Dragon writers are George Bernard Shaw and Oscar Wilde; so is Lewis Carroll and, at a deeper level of brilliant madness, Friedrich Nietzsche. The creator of our modern understanding of man's mind, Sigmund Freud, was also a Dragon.

In actors, the Dragon quality of magic you can't quite put your finger on can be seen in James Cagney, Bing Crosby, Laurence Harvey and John Gielgud; all of them understate their performances, yet capture your attention.

Getting On with Others

Here's how the Dragon people tend to harmonise—or conflict—with other Years: —

With other Dragons: Can be the most marvellous meeting of true minds, but one man's uniqueness can be the other's eccentricity.

With Rats: A very good relationship, especially at a mental level. It may not go very deep, but lots of compatibility.

With Oxen: They're intrigued by you, while you respect their practical good sense. Both of you can be stubborn when pressed.

With Tigers: They tend to be more outgoing and vain than you, while you are more perverse and uncooperative.

With Rabbits: You dislike their lack of adventure, yet

44

know in your heart of hearts that they provide the peace you crave for.

With Snakes: You can make a formidable combination, but your joint deviousness very often works against your best interests.

With Horses: In business and public affairs you work well together. In marriage the combination is fine so long as one of you is boss.

With Sheep: They find you unreliable and a bit too much of a loner, yet you make a good team if you're prepared to see each other's virtues.

With Monkeys: A wonderful partnership, so long as you don't get on each other's nerves. Both of you are restless, so need a change . . . from each other!

With Cocks: They can seem bullies, while you are tricky and unstraightforward to them. Yet it can be an enterprising, never dull relationship.

With Dogs: Here's your *bête noire*, with so much to offer them that they lack, and vice versa, that you're really meant for each other!

With Boars: Their solid strength appeals, so does their mental alertness. Excellent in an artistic, creative partnership.

YEAR OF THE SNAKE

Dates

    30 January 1881 — 17 February 1882
    17 February 1893 — 5 February 1894
     4 February 1905 — 24 January 1906
    23 January 1917 — 10 February 1918
    10 February 1929 — 29 January 1930
    27 January 1941 — 14 February 1942
    14 February 1953 — 3 February 1954
     2 February 1965 — 21 January 1966
    18 February 1977 — 7 February 1978

Your Basic Character

Your mission in life is to devote yourself entirely to the one activity/person/belief that is 'meant' for you. You have a deep inner certainty that there is this great inner task waiting for you, and your strong, pent-up emotional energy longs to find the outlet that is its destiny. Until you find your mission, you can be most difficult: chip-on-the-shoulder, self-critical, a nuisance to yourself and the rest of us.

But once this mission is found, your life is transformed.

This air of inner conflict imbues much of your attitude to life. You aren't a trivial person who can make small talk and nothing else. You have to adopt a serious approach, which needn't make you solemn but prevents you from being slapdash or permanently light-hearted.

The Years of the Snake often seem to mark climactic periods in history that are watersheds of a particular trend that then has to be reversed. Your own life is liable to be divided up into a series of clearcut episodes that seem, in retrospect, to teach a particular lesson . . . and once learnt, to bring that phase of experience to an end.

Your faults are a tendency to double-cross people, obstinacy and a seething inner temper that erupts badly when roused. Your worst enemy is yourself, for you set yourself such high standards. But although you can be a complex individual, you have a magnetism of character that is enormously appealing.

The Snake Child

The young Snake must be allowed to tackle life's problems without too protective a parental hand. He needs plenty of positive encouragement, and should be discouraged from sulking when hurt, or turning vicious when wronged. His parents and teachers in early life have a great responsibility to ensure that the child gets the right balance of discipline and independence. The key-note of his adult life is self-control, which must be voluntary rather than stemming from uptight inhibitions.

The Extrovert Snake

You'll be either an extrovert or introvert (or a bit of both, but edging towards one or the other). As an extrovert, you'll be sexy, aware of your power over others, eager to find your mission in the outer world through service, business or as a practical technologist. But even so, you'll always need to retreat into your private shell every so often.

The Introvert Snake

This shell will be very important to you, acting, as it does, as both shield and disguise. You'll find it hard to make close friends, but you'll make them for life . . . and expect a great deal from them.

Snake Activities

Typical Snake sports are mountaineering, deep-sea diving, fishing, yachting and perhaps rugby football. The emphasis must lie on personal achievement, with the Snake saying: 'This must be done . . . because I say so.'

Snake hobbies have a lonesome quality to them: reading, a solitary art form, bird-watching, amateur geology, stamp-collecting. Snakes are not desperately sociable, and prefer to concentrate their efforts in a private way. The Snake would play a solo musical instrument—say the violin—rather than partake in an orchestra.

The qualities that the Snake Year people bring to their careers are fanatical concentration, fine eye for detail, good organisational powers and the ability to take control in a crisis. They do not always mix easily with others, and may not be able to tolerate people much more stupid than themselves. Their pride makes it difficult for them to recognise that they have made a mistake—or, if they recognise it, they may not admit to it.

What Goes With Snakes

Countries believed to be associated with the Years of the Snake are Mexico, Peru, India, Saudi Arabia, Iran, Ethiopia and the USSR.

The various gems and semi-precious stones said to be connected with Snake Years are topaz, malachite, jasper, bloodstone, loadstone and flint.

Well-Known Snakes

Two politicians with a powerful sense of destiny who have both shaped the modern world to their own ends are the Snakes John F. Kennedy and Mao Tse-tung. Both combined overt honesty with behind-the-scenes deviousness.

The complex, self-torturing side of the Snake character is clearly seen in three famous writers: Dostoievsky, Conrad and, more recently, John Osborne. All three authors have created characters who were loners, set against society.

In music there's the passionate Bela Bartok; in painting, the protean Pablo Picasso. In acting, three actresses who, in their time, bewitched their audiences with the sheer power and intensity of their characterisation: Sarah Bernhardt, Mary Pickford and Audrey Hepburn.

Getting On with Others

Here's how the Snake people tend to harmonise — or conflict — with other Years: —

With other Snakes: It's either a marvellous deeply cemented love match — or a deeply cemented hate match. Depends on the Snakes involved.

With Rats: They can be a bit wishy-washy, though you're capable of developing interests in common. Dominate them!

With Oxen: Very good, except they want to build up, and you want to pull down. Accepting the differences is the start to your friendship.

With Tigers: They tend to be more extrovert than you, more volatile, more gaudy. As allies you make a formidable pair.

With Rabbits: Snakes want to be friendly with Rabbits, friendly but bossy. Funny thing is that the Rabbits often win in the long run.

With Dragons: If you're prepared to meet them halfway, you can create a really potent bond. Often, however, you're off in separate directions.

With Horses: The extrovert Horses strike you as horribly cheerful. The sensible, quiet Horses, on the other hand, make good business partners.

With Sheep: A splendid political-business partnership, only there is a clash of wills every so often. They like your courage.

With Monkeys: You're so different it isn't true—yet that's why you're so drawn towards each other. Makes a terrific pairing, if it works at all.

With Cocks: This is an excellent husband-and-wife team-up, for together you get things done fast, and can share a rich set of emotions together.

With Dogs: Fine, so long as you have the self-confidence to take control of the situation and assume leadership of the alliance.

With Boars: They complement you, but rarely compliment you. It's the animal you love to hate, and vice versa. Yet you remain fascinated by each other.

YEAR OF THE HORSE

Dates

18 February 1882 — 7 February 1883
6 February 1894 — 25 January 1895
25 January 1906 — 12 February 1907
11 February 1918 — 31 January 1919
30 January 1930 — 17 February 1931
15 February 1942 — 4 February 1943

4 February 1954 — 23 January 1955
22 January 1966 — 8 February 1967
8 February 1978 — 27 January 1979

Your Basic Character

The great thing about you is your cheerful energy. Sometimes it's too much of a good thing, turning you into a loud-mouthed bore, but by and large you have the capacity to be popular, able to spread happiness and joy wherever you go.

You do so in a slapdash, happy-go-lucky, here-today-and-gone-tomorrow sort of way. It's not that you're insensitive to other people's feelings, but your enthusiasm is like a flame in a wind, darting this way and that and settling nowhere.

Your aim in life seems to be some kind of quest, or adventure, or journey to you-know-not-where. You love finding out new facts, or discovering new opinions, or displaying new emotions as though it were the latest fashion. Always you are trying to build up a complete picture of the world — *your* world, based on your own experience. The quest is never finished, but you're the sort of person who loves travelling, hates arriving.

Your faults are tactlessness, gossiping, gambling with other people's emotions, practical joking and a sharp temper whose sharpness, of course, you have never felt because it is always directed towards other people.

Left to your own devices, you think you are happy enough, but really you miss other folks' company and, in a way, need them around to make you feel complete.

The Horse Child

He or she runs away from home very early, though usually returns in time for tea. They're adventurous, inquisitive, easily trained so long as you respect their human dignity. At school they often prove good at foreign languages, literature, and sports. They are generous to a fault, but need to be taught how other people feel—left to themselves, they are somewhat self-centred.

The Extrovert Horse

You'll be either an extrovert or introvert (or a bit of both, but edging towards one or the other). As an extrovert—and most Horses are— you'll find it simple to make friends, will be drawn to the practical side of life, will prefer a belly laugh to a chuckle, decoration to art, and an ingenious, workable answer to a lot of high-flown theory.

The Introvert Horse

You'll be the wise old fellow in the corner, a fund of fantastic stories and items of information. You seem at home with yourself, but secretly you may be a bit lonesome and wish you didn't talk to yourself so much.

Horse Activities

Typical Horse sports are all forms of athletics, especially running and javelin throwing; blood sports (not for the blood, just the thrill of the chase); Rugby League football; and of course all forms of horse-riding. Horse people really are quite sporty.

Horse hobbies tend to be open-air activities—anything from kite-flying to model-boat racing. They cannot resist turning an ordinary activity into a game, a competition —even if it's only in the mind. Typical Horse instruments in an orchestra are clarinets.

The qualities that the Horse Year people bring to their careers are zest, inventiveness, good organisational sense and the ability to put ideas across with verve and persuasion. You should aim to work in a free-wheeling, spur-of-the-moment atmosphere with plenty of the opposite sex around.

What Goes with Horses

Countries believed to be associated with the Years of the Horse are Rumania, Algeria, Austria and Libya. It's possible that Indonesia and the Lebanon are also Horse localities.

The various gems and semi-precious stones said to be connected with Horse Years are carbuncle, turquoise, amethyst, topaz and hyacinth.

Important inventions made during Horse Years have been perspex, the photographic flash bulb and magnetic tape.

Well-Known Horses

In religious fervour—Billy Graham; in the art of presenting music with passion—Leonard Bernstein; in political vision allied to energetic hilarity—Nikita Khrushchev . . . each of these men typify the Horse character in action. Think of the actor Kirk Douglas; he nearly always plays Horse personalities, perhaps because he's one himself. Think of Greta Garbo, an example of the Horse introvert—adventurous, independent, always travelling away from cosy familiarity.

The composer Igor Stravinsky exemplified the artist in search of new forms to express the rich tapestry of his feelings. Sam Goldwyn, head of MGM in its golden days, illustrated the Horse who could never say 'No' to the next impossible dream.

Getting On with Others

Here's how the Horse people tend to harmonise—or conflict—with other Years: —

With other Horses: Pretty well, though in a marriage you'll always have to respect the other's need for some independence.

With Rats: The clash comes here. From the Rat you'll learn manners, style and charm—while you can teach the Rat how to enjoy life.

With Oxen: With your zeal and their *nous*, you're bound to go far. But it's dullsville unless you can liven old Oxie up.

With Tigers: Bags of compatibility, because you're both so vital, vigorous . . . and vain! It's a firework of a relationship.

With Rabbits: You seem to bring out the beast in quiet little Rabbit. Suddenly Rabbit wants to compete on your terms . . . and can win!

With Dragons: They can twist you round their little finger . . . if they ever catch you in the first place. They're smart, you're fast!

With Snakes: So different it's laughable, but you find the Snake a fascinating creature. You're playing with fire here!

With Sheep: A friendly link between you, even though you feel that the Sheep hide more than they need, and need more than they pretend to want.

With Monkeys: They seem like you on the surface, but in the last resort you are more reliable, more robust, more realistic.

With Cocks: Many similarities between you, but it's a battle of wills that can lead to inner tensions and outer disagreements.

With Dogs: Lots of real sympathy between your two approaches to life. Can be the basis for a lasting friendship.

With Boars: Quite a few common points, but Boar is more lazy than you, while you are more slapdash than Boar.

YEAR OF THE SHEEP

Dates

     8 February 1883 — 28 January 1884
    26 January 1895 — 13 February 1896
    13 February 1907 — 1 February 1908

1 February 1919—20 January 1920
18 February 1931— 6 February 1932
5 February 1943—25 January 1944
24 January 1955—11 February 1956
9 February 1967—29 January 1968

Your Basic Character

You are a social, political, community-minded creature whose main motive in life is to succeed in commerce. Even if your work is miles removed from the world of business, you are still madly ambitious; and even if you have no work at all, you still run your life in a crisp, efficient way.

At your best, you know how to handle people, how to reach sensible, middle-of-the-road decisions, how to be wise. At your worst, you're a boot-licker and time-server with a limited outlook.

You aren't a trivial person, and seem far more intent on the basic structure of an idea than the mere decoration on top. You've a good practical mind, and even when you're being artistic, you still keep your imagination firmly rooted in reality.

Despite your ambition, not many Sheep reach the top; it seems there's somewhere a lack of drive that keeps you from the summit of your profession.

Admittedly you have staying-power, but it's the power that keeps you in line for the pension—in short, you aren't very adventurous. As far as emotional relationships are concerned, there's a wall around your heart, and only a few very special people are allowed to enter the private sanctum. As you get older, your attitudes harden and become stricter, and your potential fault is that you become square and uncompromising.

But you are a fund of realistic advice, and people respect your principles.

The Sheep Child

The young Sheep takes pleasure in personal achievement, liking encouragement but not actual help. He may

54

not be terribly demonstrative, but once he's got used to a situation, he likes to join in communal activities with other children. At school he's a plodder, thorough but a bit slow at first. He prefers a few close friends to a wide circle of acquaintances. Family life means a lot to him; later on, he'll want to become independent, but in his early years he needs an unobtrusive security.

The Extrovert Sheep

You'll be either an extrovert or introvert (or a bit of both, but edging towards one or the other). As an extrovert, you'll enjoy fairly cynical, worldly-wise conversation; you'll be active in neighbourhood clubs; you'll want to play your part in local government or voluntary work. There'll be a bluff, open attitude towards other people, even though you'll always want to reserve some part of your personality to yourself.

The Introvert Sheep

As an introvert—and most Sheep tend in this direction —you'll think before speaking, examine people carefully before making friends with them, and secretly worry about what other people are thinking of you.

Sheep Activities

Typical Sheep sports are team games of all descriptions, badminton and squash, swimming and gymnastics.

Sheep hobbies are largely indoor ones: chess and other board-games, interior decor, craftwork especially in wood, and a little quiet writing. Out-of-doors, the Sheep people like to be practical, so that even on the beach they have to build dams, castles and other sandy constructions.

The qualities that the Sheep Year people bring to their careers are common-sense based on experience, tact, logic and the ability to make unpleasant decisions. You make a good administrator, engineer, town planner, architect. You can be quite good at helping other people with practical problems, even though you keep your emotional distance from their distress.

What Goes with Sheep

Countries believed to be associated with the Years of the Sheep are Germany and Scotland (both industrious, undemonstrative nations), Poland and Czechoslovakia, Sweden, Iraq, Laos, and possibly Columbia and Greenland.

The various gems and semi-precious stones said to be connected with Sheep Years are white onyx, moonstone, jet, sapphire and perhaps jade.

The steamroller—slow but steady—was aptly invented in a Sheep Year. The famous American Monroe Doctrine, telling the 19th-century European powers to keep their hands off the other side of the Atlantic, illustrates the Sheepish desire to maintain a proper distance between people.

Well-Known Sheep

The former British Prime Minister Clement Attlee, noted for his punctilious efficiency and delight in getting things, admirably illustrates the Sheep as politician. The architect Walter Gropius, whose austere skyscrapers are classic not romantic, is a typical artistic Sheep—so is the poet Wystan Auden, whose understated definition of poetry is 'memorable prose'.

Two famous women, Margot Fonteyn and Leslie Caron, show the precise, slightly brittle charm of Sheep beauties.

Getting On with Others

Here's how the Sheep people tend to harmonise—or conflict— with other Years: —

With other Sheep: Excellent for both pleasure and business. You keep to yourselves, yet are affable in company.

With Rats: Very well in certain respects, only the Rat

oily charm irritates the plain-spoken Sheep. You are the stronger partner.

With Oxen: You're so alike in some ways, so different in others. You can't stand their bovine stubbornness, they your lamb-like sense of duty.

With Tigers: If there's enough respect on both sides, you can get on famously. But you're very different sorts of individual.·

With Rabbits: Lots of compatibility. They relax you, you inspire them. Together you make a formidable team —people can't part you.

With Dragons: They may be too quick and original for your traditional tastes. But you still rather like each other.

With Snakes: Provided you are both willing to work at the relationship, it can prove successful. Left to itself, it will develop problems.

With Monkeys: Nobody can pretend you are similar people, but there can still be mental and emotional rapport with an adult Monkey.

With Cocks: It's a battle which one of you will attain dominance. There can be lots of attraction between you.

With Dogs: Ordinary dogs love chasing sheep, but human Dogs happily play second fiddle to your leadership. A placid family link.

With Boars: Best of all mixtures, in certain ways. Boars don't make demands on you, while you have good mental rapport with them.

YEAR OF THE MONKEY

Dates

29 January 1884 — 14 February 1885
14 February 1896 — 1 February 1897
 2 February 1908 — 21 January 1909
21 January 1920 — 7 February 1921
 7 February 1932 — 25 January 1933

26 January 1944 — 12 February 1945
12 February 1956 — 30 January 1957
30 January 1968 — 16 February 1969

Your Basic Character

Too clever by half, constantly adapting your position because you're easily bored, restless and versatile and ineffably superficial—you are the highly-strung, excitable and adorably awful kind of person who's the life and soul of the party long after the party's over.

Your worst points are your untrustworthiness, slapdash methods, lack of stamina . . . and even your lying, cheating ways at times. Your good side includes your marvellous powers of persuasion, your good humour, nimble mind and ability to shrug off personal disasters and move on to the next opportunity.

In the last resort, Monkey people find it hard to grow up. J. M. Barrie, who wrote *Peter Pan*, was a Monkey, and there's something of the boy-wonder Peter Pan in all of you. You try to avoid ultimate sole responsibility; you find it a little hard to play the father figure or deeply maternal role—or rather, you can *play* these roles, like a part in a play, but rarely truly embody them.

Points of principle are far less attractive to you than points of debate. Duty, obedience, moral certainties—all these count for little in your psychology, which is more concerned with personal fulfilment, inquisitiveness and ethical options that can be kept wide-open until the last possible moment.

Think of the Monkey leaping from branch to branch of the Tree of Knowledge (or the Tree of Good and Evil) and you get a symbolic image of your restless, questing spirit.

The Monkey Child

The young Monkey is alert, agile and very much alive, but gets insecure unless protected by a safe environment. Not very brave unless very sure of the company he's keeping, he is enormously awake to the possibilities around the corner, or over the hill. At school he excels in everything—or nothing, if he's lazy. Usually he's good at exams, even if he does no revision.

The Extrovert Monkey

You'll be either an extrovert or introvert (or a bit of both, but edging towards one or the other). As an extrovert—and most Monkeys are—you'll be immensely sociable, easily mixing with all classes and types of humanity. You take things at face value, questioning their surface appearance but not their underlying meaning.

The Introvert Monkey

You'll be clever, resourceful and witty—to yourself. You'll put things down on paper rather than confide them verbally to others. You seem more profound than other Monkeys ... a bit of a scientist or philosopher.

Monkey Activities

Typical Monkey sports are fives, basketball, table-tennis —anything where nimble dexterity counts.

Monkey hobbies again require the agile use of hands: piano playing, mobile sculpture, puppetry, clay-modelling. Monkeys are not really out-of-doors people, preferring the city to the countryside, the boulevard to the bank where the wild thyme grows.

The qualities that the Monkey Year people bring to their careers are marvellous gifts of persuasion, plenty of ideas, good adaptability when it comes to changing your mind. You operate best in journalism, sales, politics, advertising.

What Goes with Monkeys

Countries believed to be associated with the Years of the Monkey are the United States and Vietnam (remember the Tet offensive in 1968, the start of the last Monkey Year), Portugal and Hungary, the Sudan and Egypt (the

Hungarian revolt and the Suez invasion took place in 1956, another Monkey Year), Cambodia and Morocco.

The various gems and semi-precious stones said to be connected with Monkey Years are crystal, aquamarine, agate, marble, topaz, beryl and chrysolite.

Inventions, discoveries and new developments of the Monkey Years form into a similar pattern, all to do with communications, speed and new ways of thinking about the fundamental properties of matter: public broadcasting, the visual telephone, radio astronomy, four-dimensional geometry, the sub-machine gun.

Well-Known Monkeys

Two 20th-century politicians offer contrasting views of the Monkey personality. Nelson Rockefeller, Governor of New York, has all the charm and quick-witted appeal of the extrovert Monkey; Oswald Mosley, leader of the pre-war British Fascists, embodies the oratorical trickery of the inner-oriented Monkey.

Typical Monkey writers are W. S. Gilbert, witty librettist of the Gilbert-and-Sullivan musical comedies, Max Beerbohm and Damon Runyon. All of them put style before content, humour before wisdom. The same pattern can be seen in Monkey actors such as comedian Ian Carmichael and lightweight Rex Harrison—perhaps, too, in the elf-like, never-to-grow-up image of singer Petula Clark. Many would think that Ian Fleming, creator of James Bond, was a Monkey driven to live in an adolescent fantasy.

Getting on with Others

Here's how the Monkey people tend to harmonise—or conflict—with other Years: —

With other Monkeys: As well as any two schoolboys—full of enthusiasm, jokes, snide remarks, envy, competition and affection.

With Rats: Very well, so long as you're prepared to

let the relationship take its course without a lot of prodding.

With Oxen: You find them steady but dull, they find you stimulating but unreliable. A good mix if you both accept your limitations.

With Tigers: Known as the kiss-me-kill-you relationship, when a love bite turns into a plain, simple bite. Plenty of fireworks between you!

With Rabbits: You're too quick for them, but every little boy needs a mother, and Rabbits are very good at tea and sympathy.

With Dragons: Very compatible indeed, for you can establish good mental companionship and smile at every disappointment.

With Snakes: You both wriggle—you with restlessness at Snake's stubborn pride, he with embarrassment at your superficiality.

With Horses: No problems so long as you're both honest with each other. But Horse hates you double-dealing, while you resent his ego-building.

With Sheep: Good for business, very different in your emotional natures. In the last resort, there's a coldness in Sheep you can't sympathise with.

With Cocks: They treat you as small fry, you try to compete, and the consequence is that it's a sizzling relationship.

With Dogs: Not nearly as bad as you might expect. Old Doggie has his good points if you'll hang around long enough to learn them.

With Boars: Some similarities in your respective natures, but lots of antipathy, too. A real ding-dong marriage here.

YEAR OF THE COCK

Dates

15 February 1885 — 7 January 1886

2 February 1897 — 21 January 1898
22 January 1909 — 9 February 1910
 8 February 1921 — 6 February 1922
26 January 1933 — 13 February 1934
13 February 1945 — 1 February 1946
31 January 1957 — 18 February 1958
17 February 1969 — 5 February 1970

Your Basic Character

Your most engaging quality is your pioneering spirit—your eagerness to see over the far side of the horizon and to broaden your mind through reading, talking and exploring. Your most despicable side is your bullying, boasting nature, your temper and sarcasm and desire to beat everyone to smithereens. Between these two extremes you veer—one moment the independent operator living off your own high-powered nervous energy, the next a small-minded person almost needing other people around in order to score points off them.

Inevitably you have a lively, forceful sexuality that warms but also threatens; there's this tendency for you to hurt those that you most love.

Your aim in life is achievement. Although you are practical, you invest it with a rare imagination that needs to glamorise ordinary life. Cocks are not often very profound theorists, or ethereal dreamers, but people of muscle who crave an element of romance to give an air of poetry to their deeds.

You lack subtlety, and devious people can easily fool you. You find it hard to laugh genuinely—kindly—at yourself, and this can lead to self-importance that is more than a little pompous. At best, you have verve and confidence, and marvellous aspirations. At worst, you're a selfish egocentric.

The Cock Child

The young Cock is not really self-conscious, so often doesn't realise what effect he is having on others. Only as an adult does the natural charm become a little calculated; as a boy or girl, the Cock is vivacious, cheeky, adventurous and keen to run his or her own life. He is not particularly gifted at academic subjects (though there are always exceptions), preferring sports and social activities to a nose in a textbook.

The Extrovert Cock

You'll be either an extrovert or introvert(or a bit of both, but edging towards one or the other). As an extrovert—and most Cocks are—you're friendly, able to understand the facts of a situation, pretty self-assured and very keen to impress your personality on the world at large.

The Introvert Cock

You're a curious mixture—an inner-oriented person with an outer-oriented character. This can lead to frustration, and cries that nobody understands you. It's only with experience and courage that you are prepared to face the world with equanimity.

Cock Activities

Typical Cock sports are fencing, boxing, wrestling—all those sports where one man faces another . . . and may the best one win. But Cocks are great sportsmen, and enjoy any form of healthy, competitive fun.

Cock hobbies are based very much on accomplishment in a practical sphere, be it making a useful object or impressing others in a social situation. These include amateur show-biz theatricals, singing and dancing, metal crafts and do-it-yourself work and, mainly for the ladies, creating a somewhat jazzy decor for the home.

The qualities that the Cock Year people bring to their careers are fine gifts of leadership (so long as other people will respect this leadership) and a sense of bounce that enables you to recover from setbacks. You operate best in fields where courage, enterprise and nerve are called for . . . and where the prize is personal prestige.

What Goes with Cocks

Countries believed to be associated with the Years of the Cock are England and Australia, the West Indies including Haiti, and possibly Ghana and Paraguay.

The various gems and semi-precious stones said to be connected with Cock Years are diamond, ruby, carbuncle and topaz.

Well-Known Cocks

In public life, two Britons capture the essence of the Cock character: Prince Philip, racy and outspoken, sporty and somewhat bossy; and former Prime Minister Anthony Eden, debonair to the point of self-love, ambitious, one of Nature's gentlemen. You can see the same story, or something like it, in two other moustachio'd heroes worshipped by many, not least themselves: actors Erroll Flynn and Douglas Fairbanks, Junior.

In music, the great 19th-century giants of opera, Wagner and Verdi, were both Cocks. And there's a similar amalgam of virility and melodrama in D. H. Lawrence. That brilliantly expressive dancer and choreographer Robert Helpmann is another Cock.

So, for that matter, is the mysterious figure Pope Paul VI—clearly an introvert Cock who has attained the highest position in his chosen vocation.

Getting On with Others

Here's how the Cock people tend to harmonise—or conflict—with other Years: —

With other Cocks: Can two people share the same throne? It can be a brilliantly successful partnership, but think of the pitfalls!

With Rats: Equals but opposites. You both have ambition, but while Rat uses charming guile, you use blatant glamour.

With Oxen: Good for a marriage so long as each partner recognises the weak points of the other . . . and refuses to exploit them.

With Tigers: You have more energy than Tiger, but both of you are made for receiving affection, not so much for giving it.

With Rabbit: You make good parents, each providing complementary gifts to your offspring. But you have much to learn from each other, too.

With Dragons: Both of you have ambitions, but Dragon is always looking for originality, you for straightforward, old-fashioned glory.

With Snakes: You take things at face value, Snakes need to worry about their inner meaning. Can make a wily business partnership.

With Horses: A great deal in common with each other, which doesn't lead to happiness! You get on fine so long as you have a rest from each other.

With Sheep: A lack of sympathy between your different aims in life, but by recognising the other person's strengths you can learn to like each other.

With Dogs: You're too flamboyant and eager in character for steady Dogs—but at least you wake them up and keep them alive.

With Boars: You have more courage, they have a sense of fair play. You have boundless energy, they like to enjoy the creature comforts.

YEAR OF THE DOG

Dates

    8 January 1886 — 23 January 1887
22 January 1898 — 9 February 1899
10 February 1910 — 29 January 1911
 7 February 1922 — 14 February 1923
14 February 1934 — 3 February 1935
 2 February 1946 — 21 January 1947
19 February 1958 — 7 February 1959
 6 February 1970 — 26 January 1971

Your Basic Character

You could fail as leader, but you're a fabulous second-in-command—loyal, dependable, thorough in your work, generous in your praise of others. There's a plodding side that others may find too narrow and limiting; but it's better to know your limits (so you think) than take stupid risks.

Your sense of humour tends to be wry, quiet and gentle; your whole attitude towards other folk is one of patient care and long-term togetherness. You cannot lose your temper easily; this proves a defect on occasion, because you don't know what to do with your excess emotion—it stays inside, troubling you. As a friend to others—and by and large, you are friendly towards most people—you are dependable and comforting, like a well-worn armchair.

The Years of the Dog are the equivalent of the dog days of summer: long, slow, essentially conservative periods of history when the mood is nostalgic rather than radical. In unassuming, hardly noticeable ways, things get consolidated and bedded down, like a dog laboriously circling his chosen resting-place before settling for a snooze.

Your great strength is this air of dependability that you exude, especially from middle-age on. People find you an easy soul to live with, an upholstered presence that can take the strain without noticing the effort.

The Dog Child

The young Dog may not see further than the end of his nose, but finds a world of pleasure in the close, familiar sights of his everyday environment. He's not particularly adventurous, shows a willingness to learn from people with experience, has a lovable, cuddly disposition, and likes to practise a skill until he's mastered it.

The Extrovert Dog

You'll be either an extrovert or introvert (or a bit of both, but edging towards one or the other). As an extrovert, you'll enjoy other people's company; you'll like listening to their stories, sharing their problems and not worrying too much about your own troubles. You're keen to show the world what you can do, though you are still not a very ambitious individual, and will settle for the comfortable middle slopes rather than the absolute summit of the mountain.

The Introvert Dog

You'll want to spend a good deal of time by yourself. You're not so certain of your place in the world, and need a good deal of encouragement from others before you play a leading role in the community. Still friendly, but you don't seem to need company so much as the extrovert Dog.

Dog Activities

Typical Dog sports are sailing, weight-lifting, long-jumping, tug-of-war. Dogs like to share their pleasures with their friends, and enjoy a bit of competition so long as it's not too strenuous.

Dog hobbies need to be stretched over a long period of time to reap their full benefit: gardening, elaborate mechanical construction kits, huge tapestries or embroideries, extensive interior modifications to the house that keep the place in dusty bedlam for months. Dogs are also scrupulous about three coats of paint. Very thorough creatures, even in play.

The qualities that the Dog Year people bring to their careers are splendid patience, organising powers and ability to maintain things as they were. You can turn your hand to almost any task that doesn't call for much imagination but, at the same time, you do tend to be underated by those around you.

What Goes with Dogs

Countries believed to be associated with the Years of the Dog are a curious mixture: Luxembourg and Malta, in Europe; Costa Rica and Guyana from the western hemisphere; Angola and Guinea, in Africa; and Korea.

The various gems and semi-precious stones said to be connected with Dog Years are pink jasper, hyacinth, agate, moonstone and cornelian.

Well-Known Dogs

There aren't a great many of them, since Dogs don't hit the headlines very much. Among women Dogs there's a tradition of beauty, exemplified by Sophia Loren, Ava Gardner and Candice Bergen. Two writers demonstrate the well-worn virtues of the animal: W. Somerset Maugham and G. K. Chesterton, consummate story-tellers without a great deal of imagination between them.

And yet . . . there's obviously a mystery about Dogs. Maybe they can rise way above their normal characteristics if times demand. The great Winston Churchill, known as the Bulldog of England, was born in a Dog Year. Interestingly enough, he used to have terrible depressions which he named his Black Dog moods. Perhaps the Year of the Dog symbolised a heavy side to his personality that he didn't much like.

Getting On with Others

Here's how the Dog people tend to harmonise—or conflict—with other Years: —

With other Dogs: Dogs love to greet each other in time-honoured ways, exchange news, have a quick run, and sleep together. Are you the same?

With Rats: Their charm can cloy, but both of you are restful people looking for a life of calm, so you manage your joint affairs very well.

With Oxen: Some similarities, but the relationship

can turn boring, without enough sparks flying for real interest.

With Tigers: So long as neither gets too possessive of the other, the relationship can prosper. You're very different, very appealing together.

With Rabbits: Very good indeed, as you are both interested in staying together. But you could turn into a dull couple.

With Dragons: This is your love-hate relationship. Sometimes they're so intriguingly attractive, sometimes so infuriatingly know-alls!

With Snakes: Their approach to life is much more intense and one-track than yours, but if you like a Snake, you like him (or her) for life.

With Horses: A great deal of compatibility—this is probably the best combination in the whole of the animal cycle.

With Sheep: Again quite good, but you can worry jointly over problems that another animal could solve in a twinkling.

With Boars: Boars needle you, you bore them—but once over those difficulties, you could develop a sincere, affectionate link.

YEAR OF THE BOAR

Dates

24 January 1887—11 February 1888
10 February 1899—30 January 1900
30 January 1911—17 February 1912
15 February 1923— 4 February 1924
4 February 1935—23 January 1936
22 January 1947— 9 February 1948
8 February 1959—27 January 1960
27 January 1971—18 February 1972

Your Basic Character

Your motive in life is to dig out the truth. You may do this in a noble way: as a university researcher, say, or any kind of student—indeed, as a self-educator throughout life. Or you may do it in a muck-raking way, not as a job of work but more as a way of life. You concentrate fiercely on one thing at a time; the rest of life can look after itself —and from this obsessiveness of attitude comes a slovenly, lazy side to your nature.

Your faults include a disparaging approach towards people less clever than yourself, a tendency to grow fat (a sign of the uncaring attitude you can develop towards certain aspects of life) and to be unsystematic.

Your virtues are your righteous indignation, especially on behalf of people imprisoned in a difficult environment, and your moral weight, which may develop only as you grow older.

You can see that you are quite a complex individual, proud of your intellectual attainments but never quite simple and placid enough in your emotional commitments. You are capable of loyalty and love, but in a way you seem to need a friendly, witty companion more than a Great Passion. If you are gripped by a bigger-than-life love affair, it nonplusses you, almost against your better judgment. Certainly the Boars of this world can be sensual, and sometimes don't know when they've had enough, but the feelings still sit a little oddly on the rest of your sardonic character.

What you need to develop is emotional patience and contentment. What you have to offer is a marvellously rigorous intelligence that can invent, argue, browbeat and inspire.

The Boar Child

The young Boar benefits from an orderly upbringing that allows him scope to explore many different branches of knowledge. Like all children, he needs a stable home background, but his parents must not be surprised if he seeks to establish his independence quite early in life. He's friendly to other children, but wants to prove his superiority, even in small ways. Threats of violence never cow him; if anything, he picks up energy and courage from this kind of danger. But he doesn't look for it in the first place.

The Extrovert Boar

You'll be either an extrovert or introvert (or a bit of both, but edging towards one or the other). As an extrovert, you'll want to impress other people and play a dominant but behind-the-scenes role in public affairs. You are self-confident but not very aware of your effect on others, so can be tactless and rude and still very pleased with yourself.

The Introvert Boar

By being mainly concerned with your own feelings and attitudes, you can be uncertain how other people react to you . . . and this causes worry and anxiety. You are likely to have just a few cronies rather than a wide number of acquaintances.

Boar Activities

Typical Boar sports are ski-ing, cricket and baseball, golf and tennis.

Boar hobbies are mainly intellectual ones: crosswords, competitions, writing or amateur dramatics. Boar girls get a lot of fun out of hair styling, playing around with make-up, and wickerwork.

The qualities that the Boar Year people bring to their careers are enthusiasm, attention to detail, ingenious mental powers and reasonably good ability to reach compromises with others. You can be the back-room boffin or the managing director, but find it hard to deal with all members of the general public.

What Goes with Boars

Countries believed to be associated with the Years of the Boar are Denmark, Israel, Brazil, Afghanistan, Burma, Iceland, Malaya and Pakistan.

The various gems and semi-precious stones said to be connected with Boar Years are moss-agate, coral, lapis lazuli, beryl and alabaster.

Well-Known Boars

What have Noel Coward, Vladimir Nabokov and Duke Ellington in common? Each, in his chosen field, is a master of wit, variety of interests, pastiche and a slightly sarky-sentimental view of humanity. There, in a sentence, is the typical Boar approach to the world.

In politics, President Georges Pompidou, chain-smoking and gourmet leader of France, and Lloyd George, the Welshman who became Prime Minister of Britain but never fitted into the Establishment, illustrate the resourceful, extrovert qualities of the public-spirited Boar.

Actors Charles Laughton and Lee J. Cobb seem to exhibit the intellectual astuteness coupled with easy-going manners typical of certain Boars.

Getting On with Others

Here's how the Boar people tend to harmonise—or conflict—with other Years: —

With other Boars: Can be tricky, especially if you're trying to score off each other. An argumentative relationship, often.

With Rats: You're different creatures—quite good for you to be the brains of the outfit, Rat the charming fellow in front.

With Oxen: You are both lazy, which is something in common. There's a kind of inner freneticism in you that's at odds with the Ox character.

With Tigers: You get on quite well with each other,

although other people might not think so. It's a kind of sexy brother-and-sister relationship.

With Rabbits: A lot of compatibility here, for though you're an independent person, you need the relaxation that Rabbit can provide.

With Dragons: A really challenging possibility! Between you, you can form a marvellously stimulating partnership, but if it doesn't work out . . . watch out for those clacking tongues!

With Snakes: Your opposite number. Snake—the right Snake for you—forces you to feel the relationship in your gut.

With Horses: Not bad. Their cheerfulness gets on your nerves a bit, but you both enjoy stirring up a bit of trouble.

With Sheep: They're more hard-working than you, which can be a wonderful basis for a relationship.

With Monkeys: You can have many laughs together . . . often at each other's expense. Whether the links go deeper is a matter of opinion . . . and trial and error.

With Cocks: They really are a bit too much of a good thing, in your judgment. Lovely for an evening, hard to live with.

With Dogs: A lovely marriageable combination, this—provided you don't allow your mental holier-than-thou attitude to throw a psychological spanner in the works.

THE SECOND PATH—Your Season of Birth

Introduction

Most people have heard of the traditional Chinese two-fold division into Yin and Yang (described further on page 204). But equally all-pervading, in ancient times, was the theory of the Five Elements.

The Chinese attempted to classify all life—from people to colours, from animals to parts of the body—into five basic categories. These are the Elements, which are Wood, Fire, Earth, Metal and Water.

This division did not pretend to classify matter into five different sorts, in the way that modern physics uses the term 'element'. The Chinese were always more interested in the relationship betwen things rather than the things themselves, and their Five Element theory really attempted to describe five sorts of fundamental life processes.

As each Element was associated with a particular season, it follows that anyone born in that season partakes, to some extent, of the qualities of that Element.

The only trouble with this is that the Chinese had a variety of ways of measuring their seasons. Sometimes they linked them to the circle of animals, calling the months of Tiger and Rabbit spring, Horse and Snake summer, and so forth; but the great difficulty was trying to fit four seasons into five elements. They always had to invent a fifth season—for instance, by calling the season corresponding to Earth the sixth month between summer and autumn. I have chosen the system mentioned by Chao Wei-Pang in which each season consisted of the three months following a solstice or equinox, less 18 days. Add the five groups of 18 days together and you have your fifth season, evenly interspersed through the year.

Since this system was developed, a mere twenty-two centuries ago, the precession of the equinoxes has meant that our seasons no longer correspond with the ancient Chinese ones. Following the modern practice among astrologers of tying our calculations to the tropical, not sidereal, year, I have used the familiar starting-dates of the seasons: March 21st, June 22nd, September 23rd and December 22nd.

What You Have To Do

Find out from the following Table in which season, according to your date of birth, you were born. Remember that the characteristics and correlations given for that season refer only to one part of your personality: the type of person you are according to the cosmic fivefold division. This affects the subtle side of you: your luck, your health, and your spiritual aspirations.

TABLE
The Five Elements of the Year

Jan. 1st—March 2nd	WATER	see page 83
March 3rd—March 20th	EARTH	see page 80
March 21st—June 3rd	WOOD	see page 76
June 4th—June 21st	EARTH	see page 80
June 22nd—Sept. 4th	FIRE	see page 78
Sept. 5th—Sept. 22nd	EARTH	see page 80
Sept. 23rd—Dec. 3rd	METAL	see page 81
Dec. 4th—Dec. 21st	EARTH	see page 80
Dec. 22nd—Dec. 31st	WATER	see page 83

THE SEASON OF WOOD

Dates

Corresponds to the dates of the year March 21st–June 3rd.

Original Meaning

When the element Wood begins its reign, if the emperor does not bestow favours and great rewards, but rather allows great cutting, destroying and wounding, then he will be in danger. Should he not die, then the heir-apparent will be in danger, and someone of his family or his consort will die, or else his eldest son will lose his life.

Original Links

The Element Wood is associated with the season of Spring. To quote an old source, 'During the rise of Yu the Great, Heaven produced plants and trees that did not wither in autumn and winter. He said: This indicates that the element Wood is in the ascendant, so our colour must be green, and our affairs must be placed under the Sign of Wood'.

Wood people will find green to be a lucky colour, especially when they are feeling downcast or ill.

Wood is associated with the East. Wood people should build their houses facing the east, they should sleep with their heads towards the east, and they should greet the dawning of each new day with a glad heart.

Wood is associated with sour tastes and goatish smells. It is associated with the wind, and so Wood people receive spiritual inspiration from the rustle of a gentle breeze or the bustle of the hill-top gust.

Wood stands in the Star-Palace of the Azure Dragon. It is linked to the stars, to Jupiter, to the ruler Yu the Great. It is the lesser Yang.

It is linked with anger, with the spleen, with the eye in your head and the muscles in your body. Your sacrifices should be laid at the inner door. Sheep and scaly fishes are the creatures of Wood. Wheat is your food. Your instruments are the compasses.

Your fortunate number is eight.

The Ministry of Agriculture is linked to the Element

of Wood. When Wood rules the world, there is relaxed government.

Modern Significance

Those born during the season of Wood instinctively hold within themselves an ideal of man as the Civilised Member of Society. When they are very quiet and meditative, they will find themselves considering how necessary it is for they themselves—and, by implication, the whole world—to calm the aggressive passions, to solve problems without going to war, and to bring courtesy and politeness into public affairs and private relationships.

Their own great inner task in life is to lead a natural, simple lifestyle—however artificial the surroundings—so that they resemble a mighty oak: strong, perfectly balanced, breathing the peace of God through every leaf and sinew of their being.

THE SEASON OF FIRE

Dates

Corresponds to the dates of the year June 22nd–September 4th.

Original Meaning

When the element Fire begins its reign, if the emperor now takes hurried and hasty measures, epidemics will be caused by drought, planets will die, and the people perish.

Original Links

The element Fire is associated with the season of summer. To quote an old source, 'During the rise of King Wên of the Chou, Heaven exhibited fire, and many red birds holding documents written in red flocked to the altar of the dynasty. He said: This indicates that the element Fire is in the ascendant, so our colour must be red, and our affairs must be placed under the Sign of Fire'.

Fire people will find red to be a lucky colour, especially when they are feeling low or psychically sick.

Fire is associated with the South. Fire people should build their houses facing the south, they should sleep with their heads towards the south, and they should greet the midday sun with a glad heart.

Fire is associated with bitter tastes and burning smells. It is associated with the heat, and so Fire people receive spiritual inspiration from the warmth of the southern sun and the radiance of the divine light.

Fire stands in the Star-Palace of the Vermilion Bird. It is linked to the Sun, to Mars, to the ruler Wên Wang. It is the greater Yang.

It is linked with joy, with the lungs, with the pulse of blood through the veins and the tongue in your mouth. Your sacrifices should be laid at the hearth. Fowl and feathered birds of the air are the creatures of Fire. Beans are your food. Your instruments are the weights and measures.

Your fortunate number is seven.

The Ministry of War is linked to the element of Fire. When Fire rules the world, there is enlightened government.

Modern Significance

Those born during the season of Fire instinctively hold within themselves an ideal of man as the Questor—in search of knowledge, in search of his spiritual home. When they are very quiet and meditative, they will find themselves considering how necessary it is for they themselves—and, by implication, the whole world—to develop vision, to see beyond the immediate day-to-day needs, to pioneer new societies, new technologies and new awareness of God, and to bring warmth and affection into public affairs and private relationships.

Their own great inner task in life is to lead a strong,

self-confident lifestyle so that they resemble the sun itself: radiant with life-force, able to rekindle energy from the divine source, a flame of the cosmic spirit.

THE SEASON OF EARTH

Dates

Corresponds to the dates of the year March 3rd–March 20th, June 4th–June 21st, September 5th–September 22nd, and December 4th–December 21st.

Original Meaning

When the element Earth begins its reign, if the emperor now builds palaces or constructs pavilions, his life will be in danger, and if city-walls are built at this time, his ministers will die. (For the people should not be taken away from the fields.)

Original links

The element Earth is associated with no particular season of the year. But to quote an old source, 'During the rise of Huang Ti (the Yellow Emperor) large earthworms and large ants appeared. He said: This indicates that the element Earth is in the ascendant, so our colour must be yellow, and our affairs must be placed under the Sign of Earth'.

Earth people will find yellow to be a lucky colour, especially when they are feeling depressed or ill.

Earth is associated with the centre. Earth people should live in houses looking in on themselves, they should sleep in the centre of the bedroom, and they should live each and every minute of the day with a glad heart.

Earth is associated with sweet tastes and fragrant smells. It is associated with the thunder, and so Earth people are spiritually cleansed by an electric storm (and may well benefit from radioactive or spiritual healing when ill).

Earth stands in the Star-Palace of the Yellow Dragon. It is linked to the planet Earth, to Saturn, to the ruler Huang Ti. It is the equal balance.

It is linked with desire, with the heart, with the mouth in your face and the flesh of your body. Your sacrifices should be laid in the inner court. Oxen and naked man are the creatures of Earth. Panicled millet is your food. Your instruments are plumblines.

Your fortunate number is five.

The affairs of the Capital city are linked to the element of Earth. When Earth rules the world, there is careful government.

Modern Significance

Those born during the season of Earth instinctively hold within themselves an ideal of man as the Centre of the Universe. When they are very quiet and meditative, they will find themselves considering how necessary it is for they themselves—and, by implication, the whole world—to lead a life of service to others, to put their needs before their own, and to reach a stoical philosophical attitude so that the desires are stilled.

Their great inner task in life is to lead just such a life of service that they resemble the pole star: steady, reliable, a beacon to those lost and frightened, their whole being revolving around the divine presence in the heart.

THE SEASON OF METAL

Dates

Corresponds to the dates of the year September 23rd–December 3rd.

Original Meaning

When the element Metal begins its reign, if the emperor attacks the mountains (by mining operations) and causes rocks to be pounded, his troops will be defeated in war, his soldiers die, and he will lose his throne.

Original Links

The element Metal is associated with the season of autumn. To quote an old source, 'During the rise of Thang the Victorious a metal sword appeared out of the water. He said: This indicates that the element Metal is in the ascendant, so our colour must be white, and our affairs must be placed under the Sign of Metal'.

Metal people will find white to be a lucky colour, especially when they are recuperating from sickness.

Metal is associated with the west. Metal people should live in houses facing the west, they should sleep with their heads towards the west, and they should bid farewell to the fading of the day in the glad hope that the sun shall rise tomorrow.

Metal is associated with acrid tastes and rank smells. It is associated with the cold, and so Metal people receive spiritual purity from the pristine snow, the crystalline ice and the bare fresh air.

Metal stands in the Star-Palace of the White Tiger. It is linked to the *hsui* constellations, to Venus, to the ruler Thang the Victorious. It is the lesser Yin.

It is linked with sorrow, with the kidneys, with the nose of your face and the skin and hair of your body. Your sacrifices should be laid at the outer door. Dogs and hairy mammals are the creatures of Metal. Hemp is your grain. Your instruments are the T-squares.

Your fortunate number is nine.

The Ministry of Justice is linked to the Element of Metal. When Metal rules the world, there is energetic government.

Modern Significance

Those born during the season of Metal instinctively hold within themselves an ideal of man as the Conveyor of Truth and Beauty. When they are very quiet and meditative, they will find themselves considering how necessary it is for they themselves—and, by implication, the whole world—to be true to their inner nature, to bring art and culture into everyday life, and to improve the quality of the environment rather than pursue selfish ends.

Their own great inner task in life is to lead a sensitive, gentle lifestyle so that they resemble a beautifully wrought silver bowl: so that they resonate when touched, and act as the vessel into which others may pour their troubles and have them eased.

THE SEASON OF WATER

Dates

Corresponds to the dates of the year January 1st– March 2nd and December 22nd–December 31st.

Original Meaning

When the element Water begins its reign, if the emperor allows the dykes to be cut, and sets the great floods in motion, his empress or great ladies will die, birds' eggs will be found to be addled, the young of hairy animals will miscarry, and pregnant women will have abortions.

Original Links

The element Water is associated with the season of winter. To quote an old source, 'Heaven will show when the time comes for the *chhi* of Water to dominate. Then the colour will have to be black, and affairs will have to be placed under the Sign of Water'.

Water people will find black, or silvery grey, to be lucky colours, especially if they are ill. Black may here correspond with the darkness of cosmic space—so deep ultramarine blue is a better modern equivalent.

Water is associated with the north. Water people should live in houses oriented to the north, they should sleep with their heads facing north, and in the stillness of the midnight hour they should honour the hidden sun.

Water is associated with salt tastes and rotten smells. It is associated with rain, and so Water people will receive spiritual refreshment from the healing showers from Heaven; they should drink rain water, and bathe in it, and imbibe the divine mercy that fertilises the human soul.

Water stands in the Star-Palace of the Sombre Warrior. It is linked to the Moon, to Mercury, to the ruler Chhin Shih Huang Ti. It is the greater Yin.

It is linked with fear, with the ear by your temple and the very marrow of your bones. Your sacrifices should be laid at the well. All grunting pigs and shell-covered invertebrates are the creatures of Water. Millet is your food. Your instruments are the scales and balances.

Your fortunate number is six.

The Ministry of Works is linked to the element of Water. When Water rules the world, there is quiet government.

Modern Significance

Those born during the season of Water instinctively hold within themselves an ideal of man as the Channel of Sympathy. When they are very quiet and meditative, they will find themselves considering how necessary it is for they themselves—and, by implication, the whole world—to act as comforting mothers to the distressed and bereaved; to have simple, honest emotions, quick to respond to the needs of others; and to love their friends and business colleagues.

Their own great inner task in life is to quell the ocean of fears within the belly; to walk upon the Sea of Tranquillity; and to bathe humanity in the eternal tears from which we have been nurtured, and to which all must return.

THE THIRD PATH—Your Fortnight of Birth

Introduction

We've seen how the ancient Chinese labelled each year with the name of an animal, and each season with a so-called element. They also had the twelve months of the calendar, which they divided into 24 segments. Half were called *chhi*-centres and half *chhi*-nodes. It's these 24 fortnights, and their meaning, which form the Third Path in our journey towards an understanding of your personality.

It's fair to add that this Third Path is a real East–West amalgamation. The Chinese, as I say, simply used these *chhi* as means of telling the time; there was no fortune-telling associated with them. But each *chhi* happens to correspond to half a Zodiacal Sign in Western astrology; so the interpretations given here are a familiar part of our traditional astrological knowledge.

What You Have To Do

Find out from the following Table what, according to your date of birth, is your Chinese *chhi* or Fortnight. Remember that your *chhi* describes only part of your personality: the kind of social and political creature you are, your attitude towards everyday work, the kind of aptitudes and talents—and maybe lack of talents! —you are likely to bring to your career, and the types of occupation that will probably suit you.

If your birthday falls right at the end or beginning of a *chhi* and you don't feel the description given suits you, go to the one beyond—or back, whichever is relevant—to see if that suits you better. The reason for this is that the dates given in the Table are the nearest possible approximations, but as we have a leap year every four years, these dates may fractionally change year by year. It also makes a little difference which time of day you were born.

TABLE OF FORTNIGHTS

1   BEGINNING OF SPRING

Origins

First of the 24 Chinese fortnightly periods, covering the dates February 5th–18th. Chinese name: *li chhun*. Meaning: the beginning of Spring. Corresponds with the second half of the Zodiacal Sign of Aquarius.

Your Place in the World

Your social and political attitudes are idealistic, humanitarian and liberal-progressive in tone. You see yourself as a member of a democracy, neither better nor worse than your fellows, but you would prefer affection and conciliation to play a greater role in public affairs than they normally do nowadays.

Your Attitude to Work

Your work in life needs to be socially useful as well as personally rewarding. Neither money nor fame are the chief spurs; you would happily take a lower salary to tackle a vocation that really fulfilled your promise as an individual. You are capable of hard work, and plenty of it, in these circumstances; but you turn bolshie if you are denied the opportunity to exercise some initiative of your own—and if you find it impossible to respect your superior at work.

Your Talents and Weaknesses

You've a good mind capable of being trained in logic even though it constantly wants to go beyond pure reason into the realm of intuition. You like working with people, but don't have to. You aren't necessarily a great leader, but can organise people in small groups and make an excellent representative like a shop steward. Ideally you're not a blue-collar so much as a white-collar worker, as you need to use your brain more than your brawn.

Certainly you are suited to technical work, though it's nice if the technology concerned has either an artistic or clearly beneficial result in the community. You need some independence, though in the last resort you're better in an enterprise with others than simply as a self-employed person.

Your main weakness is your lack of decision-making at

the right time. You tend to dither, or put off important matters until tomorrow.

Career Choices

In Industry, as a worker in quality control, telemetry, research and development, laboratory technician.

In commerce, as a sales representative of specialised goods (e.g. educational equipment, instruments), technical draughtsman, commercial photographer, printer.

In the social services, as a mental health worker, community worker in special areas such as race and grass-roots democracy (local authority, political party, trades union, registered charity, etc).

In the professions, as a (probably Jungian) psychologist, a lawyer dealing with problems of human justice, and a do-gooding politician.

2   RAIN

Origins

Second of the 24 Chinese fortnightly periods, covering the dates February 19th–March 5th. Chinese name: *yü shui*. Meaning: the rains. Corresponds with the first half of the Zodiacal Sign of Pisces.

Your Place in the World

You bring an honest-to-goodness optimism to all your social and political attitudes, though others might call it blind faith. You want to think well of all statesmen, but too much disillusion will lead to an escapist desire to live in a make-believe world—perhaps a retreat to the romance of an historical period (the 'good old days') or an imaginative utopia. You cannot bear too much reality.

Your Attitude to Work

Your immature approach to work would be totally frivolous, seeing it as an unwelcome interruption of your leisure hours. As you become more responsible, however, you're likely to adopt a caring, somewhat idealistic attitude. At the right vocation you would willingly work for no salary at all, provided your necessities were met. Two other motivations are far more powerful with you than mere money. One is the Just Cause (you love throwing yourself heart and soul into some enterprise you believe in) and the other Sympathy for Others.

Your Talents and Weaknesses

You operate through your heart more than your head, and therefore are better suited to work dealing with people rather than machines. You are not a particularly good organiser, partly because you need a strong guiding hand in a crisis but mainly because you can be so easily swayed by transient moods—to say nothing of persuasive tongues.

You probably have good artistic aptitude, whether or not it has been properly trained.

Except where personal dedication gives you the necessary will-power to concentrate, you should avoid precision work; you're better at work that can be a bit blurred at the edges!

Career Choices

In Industry, as a personnel officer, worker in oil, chemical, gas or pharmaceutical industries. (Watch out you aren't made a scapegoat by your work-colleagues.)

In commerce, as a caterer (particularly drink), shipping agent, harbour master, fishmonger.

In the social services, as a nurse or other medical worker, animal care worker including veterinarian, rodent operative or swimming bath attendant.

In the arts, almost anything—but particularly as a dancer or musician.

In the professions, a teacher of literature or the arts, marriage guidance counsellor or industrial conciliator.

Origins

Third of the 24 Chinese fortnightly periods, covering the
dates March 6th–20th. Chinese name: *ching che* or *chih*.
Meaning: the awakening of creatures from hibernation.
Corresponds with the second half of the Zodiacal Sign of
Pisces.

Your Place in the World

You are caught between dream and reality, wishful
thinking and down-to-earth respect for facts. Sometimes
you yearn for a never-never world of sweetness and light
and good nature; at other times, you live in the here-and-
now world, scoffing at foolish fancies. Your political attitudes are affected by this twin-nosed approach to the
everyday world—at one moment you are berating all
statesmen for being cynical creatures without an ounce
of human kindness, at the next you are making excuses
for them. Your own ambitions are just the same: hover-
ing between day dreams and a cheerful acceptance of the
existing situation.

Your Attitude to Work

As an immature person you're liable to get trapped in
the gulf between your impossibly high hopes as an adolescent and your realisation, a few years out of school, that
you'll have to settle for second-best. As you grow older,
you are able to blend the two strains in your character
closer together, making you a practical idealist, or workaday artist. Money and success are quite important, but
pride in your own creation comes top in your order of
priorities.

Your Talents and Weaknesses

As a young person, you are more led than leader, falling
in with other people's orders happily enough. As a

developed adult, you prefer to exercise a bit of initiative, and by middle age you want to run your own show.

You mix well with work-colleagues, and are prepared to work as a member of a team provided (a) when you are young the task in hand has a social purpose behind it, and (b) when you are older you are in charge of the team.

You combine a good imagination with clever manual skills, making you an admirable artisan in a variety of fields. You like outdoor work, where there's an illusion of freedom, or a job involving a good deal of travelling.

Career Choices

In industry, as a plumber, water engineer, hydraulics worker. You also make an admirable round-the-corner handyman-cum-builder.

In commerce, shop worker in fashion or sports departments, ship's chandler, sales representative in swimming pools, aquatic and marine gear, marine insurance broker.

In the social services, rehabilitation worker with alcoholics, ex-prisoners, ex-mental patients; occupational therapist.

In the arts, anything edging towards the crafts—potter, needleworker, decorative artist.

In the professions, engineer, mathematician.

4 SPRING

Origins

Fourth of the 24 Chinese fortnightly periods, covering the dates March 21st–April 5th. Chinese name: *chhun fen*. Meaning: the Spring Equinox. Corresponds with the first half of the Zodiacal Sign of Aries.

Your Place in the World

You view the world as a child sees a seaside beach: as a place to dam streams, fight back the advancing tide and build your own castle where you can be king. You are a conqueror, a pioneer, an independent who can look after himself. So you don't take kindly to the welfare state where so much is done for you; and you hate the bureaucratic state, which tries to stop you doing the things you want. You expect political leaders to be honest, forthright, practical people, but aren't really at home in a democracy.

Your Attitude to Work

The energy coursing through your psyche means that you work hard (and play hard)—though if the work is boring and you are trapped in uncongenial surroundings, you are capable of abruptly downing tools and leaving. Personal fulfilment is your goal in your career, which you measure in objective terms: how many bridges have I built, how big an impression have I made?

Your Talents and Weaknesses

You work with a hard-headed brain that respects facts, and a spirit that won't accept defeat. You're a highly competitive creature enjoying the rat race against co-workers and rivals in other firms. You have the will-to-win.

You fancy yourself as a leader, and other people certainly rally round you in a crisis. But just as Winston Churchill was thrown out of office after World War II, so are you liable to be ignored more than you welcome in everyday circumstances.

You're a good organiser of yourself and a dedicated band of followers, but you give orders more than you persuade.

Your faults are lack of imagination, especially into the human condition, and insensitivity in putting ideas across. Your virtues are good practical ability, quickness of thought and decision-making, courage to take risks, and a liking for machines.

Career Choices

In industry, almost anywhere, but especially civil engineering, mechanical engineering, construction work, steel worker, transport worker.

In commerce, again in a great many fields, especially economic planning, marketing or sales director, export manager.

In the social services, prison officer, police service, youth worker (especially Outward Bound and similar ventures).

In the arts, metalwork sculptor.

In the professions, the armed services, especially the Army, teacher of physical education, dentist, surgeon, barrister.

5   **CLEAR AND BRIGHT**

Origins

Fifth of the 24 Chinese fortnightly periods, covering the dates April 6th–20th. Chinese name: *chhing ming*. Meaning: clear and bright. Corresponds with the second half of the Zodiacal Sign of Aries.

Your Place in the World

As a young man or woman, you have the energy and enterprise to get what you want. The older you get, however, the more you will slow down, preferring routine to adventure, settled conditions to being constantly on the move. In your social and political views, you gradually veer in the course of your life from a self-sufficient belief in the power of the individual to a more mellow desire for shared security. You start off as a radical Tory, so to speak, and become an Establishment conservative.

Your Attitude to Work

A natural worker, even in leisure pursuits, you enjoy

purposive activity. Your goals vary, according to your age. As a youngster you need the thrill of personal endeavour and success; as a middle-aged square, you prefer the quieter aims of financial prosperity and respectability, together with some authority at work.

Your Talents and Weaknesses

You bring quite a dare-devil, gambling quality to your early career. Later, this merges into a more steady, perservering approach. Again, as a young person you are inventive, courageous and fast-thinking, while by middle age you've become a creature of routine, less agile in your ideas but capable of deeper, profound thought.

Throughout your life, you are a realist, practical in outlook and application. As you grow older, however, you'll become more in tune with the needs of other people —though it's fair to say that you never lose a natural self-interest.

You're an admirable organiser, in the office or on the factory floor or, for that matter, on the building site. People trust you to finish a job on time (though as a youngster you'll dart from venture to venture in a slightly slapdash way).

Career Choices

In industry, as a steeplejack or steel erector, fitter, welder, especially in the building trade. Not suited to production line work until middle age.

In commerce, as a property entrepreneur, stock market analyst, sales representative (especially in musical instruments, real estate, life assurance).

In the social services, adventure playground supervisor, teacher of biological sciences, physics, geology.

In the arts, stonemason or sculptor in marble.

In the professions, as a soldier, engineer sportsman or woman.

6 GRAIN RAIN

Origins

Sixth of the 24 Chinese fortnightly periods, covering the dates April 21st–May 5th. Chinese name: *ku yü*. Meaning: grain rain. Corresponds with the first half of the Zodiacal Sign of Taurus.

Your Place in the World

At best you have a splendid steady self-assurance that suggests you stand four-square in the centre of the universe, and the world revolves around you. You like to build towards a position of trust and respectability in your career and in society. You are a natural conservative, wanting to keep the best of the past and advancing fairly cautiously into radical policies. You expect your statesmen to be, above all, reliable and safe men, especially in matters of defence and finance.

Your Attitude to Work

Work comes easily to you once you are properly motivated for it. Your priorities are, first and foremost, the desire for economic security (so a steady income is preferable to a high-risk venture), pride in your own accomplishments, approval from others in terms of recognised success. Relatively low are the motives to help others and the community-at-large.

As you get older, you can get lazy—and if the habit develops early, you may never fulfil your real potential.

Your Talents and Weaknesses

Your great strength is your dependability. You need a job where you have responsibility. Your weakness is a relative lack of mental agility, so that fast-talking, quick-thinking situations don't suit you.

You are good at maintaining an existing arrangement

rather than creating a brand-new one. Once you have learnt a rule, you stick by it, even if conditions change, so you lack flexibility of outlook. You are not a natural leader, making a much better No Two.

Thus you make an excellent organiser and administrator, especially of financial, legal and governmental affairs.

At a manual level, you certainly have the strength and resilience to work hard in fairly humble employment. Ideally, however, in even the most monotonous of work, you require some element of artistry in what you do.

Career Choices

In industry, as a manual labourer or semi-skilled trades, as the routine doesn't easily bore you. In the construction business, in farming and market gardening, in soil management, ecology and the environment.

In commerce, as a civil servant or office worker in a large institution or public company, in the middle reaches of administrative management, as a banker, accountant, economist, book-keeper, etc. As a maintenance worker, storeman, shop assistant, property developer.

In the social services, as a park keeper, gardener, social security worker.

In the arts, as a clay-modeller, potter, writer.

In the professions, as an auctioneer, architect or surveyor.

7   SUMMER

Origins

Seventh of the 24 Chinese fortnightly periods, covering the dates May 6th–21st. Chinese name: *li hsia*. Meaning: the beginning of Summer. Corresponds with the second half of the Zodiacal Sign of Taurus.

Your Place in the World

You combine a feeling for security with a need **for** versatility. One part of your nature likes to be settled—to know where you stand—while another part needs a spice of adventure.

So you see yourself as a solid citizen with the breadth of mind to understand the other fellow's point of view. In your social and political views, you are a moderate right-winger who will probably become more flexible in outlook as you gain experience. You like your statesmen to be sensible chaps, and you're a great admirer of good oratory.

Your Attitude to Work

You enjoy work when you have to do it, but you aren't quite as full of stamina as you like to think and there's an increasing tendency for you to leave a job half-finished if a new interest crops up. Financial reward is important to you, not out of a sense of greed but a sense of responsibility towards your dependants. You like saving money, and taking out life policies, and it's this that keeps you in steady employment more than an overwhelming desire to be a success.

Your Talents and Weaknesses

You are richly endowed with financial acumen, commonsense and practical outlook on life. At worst, this can become a wholly materialistic approach, for there's little of the idealist about you. At best, you get things done—not very quickly, but usually thoroughly.

You also have a good artistic sense—of form, colour and harmony—which may come through in your life's work. You can put your ideas across quite well, especially after you've had a bit of practice.

Your weakness is lack of initiative. You prefer someone else to take the risks, or give the orders. You make a fine second-in-command.

Career Choices

In industry, in transportation of heavy goods, in factory maintenance, stores control, mechanical engineering, machine operator.

In commerce, in all kinds of financial processes, especially mortgages and hire purchase deals; in the Civil Service, especially dealing with housing; in administrative fields to do with various manufacturing processes including caravans, parks and gardens, domestic equipment, agricultural goods, etc.

In the social services, especially pensions.

In the arts, as a singer or musician, writer, painter or 'kinetic' artist.

In the professions, as an archaeologist (especially industrial paleontologist, geologist, ecologist, organic chemist.

8   LESSER FULLNESS

Origins

Eighth of the 24 Chinese fortnightly periods, covering the dates May 22nd–June 6th. Chinese name. *hsiao man*. Meaning: the lesser fullness of grain. Corresponds with the first half of the Zodiacal Sign of Gemini.

Your Place in the World

Your attitude towards the world resembles that of a small boy in a garden; there are so many things to do, so many places to explore, that you can't be bothered to concentrate on any one in particular. You remain a youngster at heart throughout life, never quite growing up and therefore never quite assuming your rightful place as a responsible, upright citizen.

You believe in a free, open society where everyone shares in the decision-making process. You dislike too much authority, and lack strong principles yourself, even though you enjoy laying down the law in arguments. You respond to politicians who are flexible in outlook.

Your Attitude to Work

Work is really a game to you. So long as it's fun, you enjoy it; as soon as it turns serious and effortful, you start looking for more amenable employment. What really motivates you is the stimulation that comes from work: the excitement of new developments, the exchange of information, the cut-and-thrust of argument and business rivalry.

Your Talents and Weaknesses

You're the perfect ideas man: full of bright notions, but lacking the commonsense and judgment to make the final decision. You function well in research departments, information centres, schools and colleges and the communications media. Since your greatest asset is your quickness of mind coupled with your ability to organise your thoughts into persuasive arguments, you also make a good salesman.

You lack the ability to organise very effectively, partly because you aren't thorough enough and partly owing to your relative inability to make an overall plan. You tend to work piecemeal.

You tend to give way under pressure, and cannot be depended on in a crisis.

Career Choices

In industry, as a transport driver, bus or coach driver, railman, postman, clippie, travel agent, anyone engaged in the manufacture of transport goods, newsprint and stationery, printing equipment, etc.

In commerce, as a shop worker, waiter in hotel, telephonist, radio operator, clerk, especially in import-export or mail order business.

In the social services, speech therapist, family planning expert, work with disabled people.

In the arts, as a writer, publisher, pianist or violinist.
In the professions, as a barrister, stock broker, lecturer or teacher (especially of literature and languages).

9   GRAIN IN EAR

Origins

Ninth of the 24 Chinese fortnightly periods, covering the dates June 7th–21st. Chinese name: *mang chung*. Meaning: the grain in ear. Corresponds with the second half of the Zodiacal Sign of Gemini.

Your Place in the World

At the outset you're a lively, inquisitive individual liking to remain a free agent; but the older you get, the more you want to settle down and feel you belong to a particular family, home town, political affiliation and set of principles.

You believe in full discussion of issues, and so favour a democratic society in which you have a right to voice your opinion and affect policy to some extent. As a young person you change your social and political ideas a good deal, but by middle age you tend to come down on the conservative side of the fence.

Your Attitude to Work

You're not the world's hardest worker. You're goaded into it partly, in your youth, by a sense of excitement at tackling a new project and partly, when you grow older, by your inner need for security (emotional as well as financial).

You appreciate the applause of others for work well done, but don't really want so much success that you're loaded down with responsibilities.

Your Talents and Weaknesses

You excel in quick, clever calculations, dexterity of thought, finding the right words for the task in hand. You are relatively poor in perseverance, courage and leadership, though the people who do follow you will tend to become friends rather than mere subordinates.

You get on well with nearly all people, but it's wise to remember that you can be spiteful to a work-colleague who seems to have done you wrong. You can also be petty about trivial debts, even though you can be slow enough paying your own debts.

You love acting as the middle-man in a transaction, as an arbitrator or messenger or conciliator. You are skilful at personal contacts of all kinds.

You should avoid routine work, though not run away from any that comes your way in the course of a more interesting job.

Career Choices

In industry, as carrier of goods, removal and cartage operator, ferry worker, airline official, courier, messenger, crane operator, production manager.

In commerce, as estate agent, domestic employment agent, door-to-door salesman, secretary (especially in a busy office), business negotiator, newspaper reporter, publisher, advertising copywriter, etc.

In the social services, work with the deaf, dumb and blind.

In the arts, as playwright, novelist, percussionist in music.

In the professions, as a divorce lawyer, teacher of economics.

Origins

Tenth of the 24 Chinese fortnightly periods, covering the dates June 22nd–July 6th. Chinese name: *hsia chih*. Meaning: the Summer solstice. Corresponds with the first half of the Zodiacal Sign of Cancer.

Your Place in the World

It's very important for you to feel wanted—in your workplace, your neighbourhood, your social community. You cannot easily step outside your society and play the loner; you need to belong.

It follows that you tend to stick to the rules laid down by society. You aren't a natural rebel, tending to conform. You're a kind of emotional conservative, valuing the past more than the future. You like your statesmen to be familiar, fireside people you can trust. If anything, you revert back to the old feudal, tugging-the-forelock days.

Your Attitude to Work

You work out of a need for security. You need the money to feel safe. But in addition, you enjoy work that seems to be building a solid, permanent enterprise and which seems to have some kind of social purpose. Although you are good at business and commerce, you flourish also in the social services and the arts. But if you were made a millionaire tomorrow, you would probably stop work altogether. It isn't that important to you.

Your Talents and Weaknesses

Your best quality is sheer human sympathy that enables you to get into the heart and mind of another person and share his or her feelings. Clearly you work well in a human situation where care and compassion are needed.

Your greatest weakness is probably your cowardice, which makes it hard for you to stand up to rough, tough people in business and to cope with noisy, difficult conditions in a factory or dockyard.

Equally you are not really suited to detailed calculations or other precise work. You need opportunities where your intuition can expand.

Career Choices

In industry, in the personnel department, in hotel and catering work, in the Merchant Navy, in food production and supply industries, in manufacturing industries dealing with domestic equipment.

In commerce, as company secretary, financial and budgetary control, company archivist, information retrieval.

In the social services, almost anywhere, but easily the most popular is nursing, followed by child care, ante- and post-natal work, child adoption officer, marriage guidance counselling, etc.

In the arts, as novelist, marine painter.

In the professions, as historian, marine biologist.

11   LESSER HEAT

Origins

Eleventh of the 24 Chinese fortnightly periods, covering the dates July 7th–22nd. Chinese name: *hsiao shu*. Meaning: the lesser heat. Corresponds with the second half of the Zodiacal Sign of Cancer.

Your Place in the World

You're a traditionalist—and proud of it. You believe in the good old virtues, in an established order, in government and law and order. But you qualify all this rigidity with an inner core of softness that insists on mercy, gentleness and old-world courtesy. You may be ambitious, but aren't a social climber. You may want security for yourself and your family, but you aren't greedy. You know your place in life, and wish to goodness others knew theirs! You like your statesmen to be cautious, just men without any frills but confident of their own judgment.

Your Attitude to Work

If there's work to be done, you set to and complete it. If there's no work, you're quite capable of occupying your time with a wide range of leisure activities. As mentioned above, what motivates you is the need for security, but you combine this with a creative urge that needs the applause of the crowd as well as self-congratulation.

Your Talents and Weaknesses

Your greatest asset is your ability to understand your fellow humans and to want to help them in their distress. You like looking after their welfare, but are less good in more mechanical, computer-like surroundings.

Your weakness is your tendency to take criticism too personally, and therefore to resent interference from above without having the guts to tell your boss where to get off! You need to work in congenial offices where there's a family feeling among the employees. You make quite a good employer yourself so long as you have a tough, shrewd second-in-command telling you when you're being too soft!

Your moods get in the way of completely smooth efficiency, so every so often your co-workers will have to make allowances for your off-days.

Career Choices

In industry, as cleaner, repairer, maintenance worker. As stockman, process engineer, house journal editor, sign-writer, anyone in maritime affairs.

In the social services, as nurse (especially in recuperation centres, cruise liners, etc), as home help, midwife, playschool teacher, primary school teacher, florist and flower arranger.

In commerce, as finance analyst, salesman of domestic goods, nursery men, groundsmen, librarians.

In the arts, muralists, home crafts, tapestry-work.

In the professions, as doctor (particularly general practitioner).

12   GREATER HEAT

Origins

Twelfth of the 24 Chinese fortnightly periods, covering the dates July 23rd–August 7th. Chinese name: *ta shu.* Meaning: the greater heat. Corresponds to the first half of the Zodiacal Sign of Leo.

Your Place in the World

Ideally you see yourself occupying an important position in society. Certainly you enjoy the idea of people paying attention to you, partly due to your wisdom, mainly owing to your personal charm and knack at handling situations that call for a firm hand. You have a powerful, self-assured vision of yourself in career and citizenship duties alike.

Your social and political views tend to be romantic-Tory. You like the idea of the strong leader whose personality can weld the nation together: a De Gaulle or Churchill or even a Kennedy. You do not really respond to democratic procedures, preferring a monarchy—even an absolute one, like the Sun King's in France—to the chaos of the masses.

Your Attitude to Work

You are a hedonist by nature, liking sunbathing a lot more than slogging at the workbench or office desk! But if you must work, then you prefer a congenial job allowing scope to use your personality. Much the most important motivation in you, as far as work is concerned, is vanity; you work to gain other people's approval, and to satisfy your own desire for glory and success.

Your Talents and Weaknesses

You aren't the cold, back-room schemer at all. To function at your best, you need to project your personality in a strong, confident manner—giving orders, spreading enthusiasm, generally running the show. This is your greatest asset and, of course, your besetting weakness as well—for the assurance turns into bombast, the pride into conceit. So some people will always find you unbearable, while to others you're a god.

You love making broadly-based plans for the future; love thinking big, setting up important deals; love being thought generous by your staff and up-and-coming by your superiors.

It's hard for you to give way in a professional argument, so you lack flexibility. And it's very hard for you to see yourself in a genuinely humble light.

Career Choices

In industry, as foreman, manager, director and preferably chairman himself!

In commerce, as 'front man' of someone else's organisation; as self-employed businessman; as window-dresser, sales assistant or receptionist; as host or hostess in night club, cabaret, etc; croupier, anyone in the holiday business.

In the social services, as physio-therapist, organiser of charitable club (particularly on the entertainments side).

In the arts, as actor or actress, anything in show-biz.

In the professions, politician, diplomat.

Origins

Thirteenth of the 24 Chinese fortnightly periods, covering the dates August 8th–23rd. Chinese name: *li chhiu.* Meaning: beginning of Autumn. Corresponds to the second half of the Zodiacal Sign of Leo.

Your Place in the World

You certainly have plenty of self-confidence and personal pride, but you combine these qualities with a shrewd, canny understanding of the way the world works. Clearly you want to be a big success, whether in your career or social position, and you have the capacity to develop the know-how to get it. (You already have the luck; you were born with it!)

You believe in a kindly, well-ordered society allowing the maximum of freedom with the minimum of fuss. You don't think people should be cosseted too much, as you like to behave in a self-reliant way yourself. Your ideal political leader has great charisma. He rules because of the person he is.

Your Attitude to Work

Your ambition is harnessed to an ability and readiness to work unstintingly. You won't work for an uncooperative employer, though you'll do a great deal for a congenial boss. Ideally, of course, you want to be boss yourself —that's your real motivation.

Your Talents and Weaknesses

Your best points are your personal charm, which should ideally be used in your work, together with an ability to think on a large scale yet still be able to cope with detail. Your weakness is a tendency to be blinded to a new idea because the old idea is yours—and whatever you do is marvellous, isn't it?

You welcome the opportunity to work with others, and make a good employee so long as the surroundings are pleasant and you have sufficient chance to use your initiative and perhaps give a few orders to underlings.

You have the courage of your convictions, the ability to hold your own in an argument, tremendous zeal for a brand-new enterprise but, if faced with real difficulties, you can get easily depressed—rather like a spoilt child at times.

Career Choices

In industry, as financial director, area organiser, power station worker, atomic energy expert, nuclear engineering.

In commerce, administrator (especially of holiday camps, guided tour companies, packaged overseas trips), greengrocers, confectionery goods dealer, bookmaker.

In the social services, sun-ray lamp operator, local authority entertainments manager, meals-on-wheels organiser.

In the arts, as jeweller and other precision-work craftsman.

In the professions, as architect, broadcaster.

14   END OF HEAT

Origins

Fourteenth of the 24 Chinese fortnightly periods, covering the dates August 24th–September 7th. Chinese name: *chhu shu*. Meaning: end of heat. Corresponds with the first half of the Zodiacal Sign of Virgo.

Your Place in the World

You're a great pigeon-holer, so you know your own place in the world only too well. You wish other people would slot into their right station in life, too, and not cause so much fuss!

You believe in a peaceful, keeping-your-nose-out-of-other-people's-business kind of world and an efficient, nononsense government. You are neither particularly radical nor especially reactionary—just pragmatic, appreciating the facts of the situation and seeing clearly what needs to be done to tidy up the mess. Statesmen, to your way of thinking, should be businesslike and unflamboyant.

Your Attitude to Work

You are one of the world's great workers, for everything you tackle, from washing-up to writing a long report, is treated by you as work . . . and you love it.

It's the sheer enjoyment of finishing a task, knowing it's been well done, that motivates you. Money, glory, the approval of friends aren't all that important, for you set your own standards and are quite aware whether or not you've worked well.

Your Talents and Weaknesses

Your greatest asset is your needle-sharp mind that is marvellous at close, detailed study. Just as you can disentangle a muddled skein of wool, so can you decipher a complex mass of facts and make sense out of them. It's the same with skilled manual work; you have fine dexterity, able to piece together intricate machine components.

Your relative weakness is your matter-of-fact coolness in dealing with other people. Not that you're cold—but occasionally, to use the immortal phrase of Nye Bevan, a desiccated calculating machine. Sometimes you treat co-workers as automata that have to fit into the existing time schedule.

You are good at paper-work and general administration, excellent with figures, not really suited for heavy, boring manual work but better in the office. You need variety, but have the stamina to stick to the job in hand.

Altogether, a model employee. Whether you have the toughness, sense of enterprise and qualities of leadership to be top man in the company is open to question.

Career Choices

In industry, all kinds of semi-skilled and skilled manual work in light industry; quality control engineering, time and motion study, factory inspectorate, laboratory technician, scientist.

In commerce, as secretary, filing clerk, accountant, anyone processing papers.

In the social services, as a nurse, keep-fit instructor, teacher, psychologist.

In the arts, as a critic.

In the professions, as a solicitor.

15   WHITE DEWS

Origins

Fifteenth of the 24 Chinese fortnightly periods covering the dates September 8th–22nd. Chinese name: *pai lu.* Meaning: white dews. Corresponds with the second half of the Zodiacal Sign of Virgo.

Your Place in the World

In your social and political attitudes, you're a mild, even timid, keeping-yourself-to-yourself individual that wouldn't hurt a fly . . . but still think flies are disgusting creatures spreading disease!

You approve of the 'nanny State' where the government acts as a nursemaid by tidying up after citizens, keeping them in order for their own good, teaching them courtesy to others and self-respect towards themselves.

You are content to play the model citizen yourself — but should you develop a grudge against society, you'd make an efficient criminal . . . probably in a sneaky misdemeanour like fraud or poisoning your spouse!

Your Attitude to Work

Obviously you adore work, especially when there's something to grumble about—or, better still, worry about secretly. It keeps you on your toes.

Anxiety keeps you alive. Have you done everything correctly? Is there a last detail you've missed? Will the boss be pleased? When will something—anything—go wrong? Worry, worry, worry—that's your big motivation.

Your Talents and Weaknesses

Your special aptitudes at work are an ability to grasp a new point quickly and be able to explain it lucidly to others. You've a fine attention to detail—perhaps too fine, as sometimes you lose sight of the forest by concentrating too single-mindedly on the individual trees.

You may be affable to your co-workers, but don't really mix as easily as you might wish. You should avoid those jobs where you need to lay on the charm with a trowel—not that you lack your own brand of charm, but you hate doing anything that grabs personal attention like that.

You have so many admirable workaday qualities that you make a fine employee. Perhaps it's fair to add that you may lack imagination—though not inventiveness—and human sympathy. But the older you get, the more mellow you become.

Career Choices

In industry, precision work (e.g. clock-making, solid-state electronics) laboratory work in medicine, chemical technology; analyst.

In commerce, as statistician, book-keeper, wages clerk, company secretary, organisation and methods worker.

In the social services, as coroner, forensic scientist, work with mentally handicapped people (also with artificial limbs).

In the arts, as etcher, print-maker, jeweller.

In the professions, as doctor (particularly a specialist).

111

Origins

Sixteenth of the 24 Chinese fortnightly periods covering the dates September 23rd–October 8th. Chinese name: *chhiu fen*. Meaning: the Autumn equinox. Corresponds to the first half of the Zodiacal Sign of Libra.

Your Place in the World

There's only one place you want to occupy: the middle of the road, neither too far left nor right, keeping a nice balance. This makes you an agreeable citizen, uncomplaining for much of the time, happy to jog along.

Obviously you believe in a fair, happy society. Justice must be tempered with mercy; unpleasant social conditions must be tidied out of sight. That's your trouble: you're a bit of an appeaser, giving in to political bullies for the sake of peace and quiet.

Your Attitude to Work

There's a lazy streak in your nature that is quite content to let other people do the hard work while you look decorative on the side. When you do tackle a job, you prefer it to be a graceful, easy sort of task that doesn't take too much out of you. So what motivates you to get off your backside and actually do some work? Well, the approval of other people counts a lot with you; you like a job that has social cachet. You also like work that brings you into contact with many other people: in short, a friendly way of passing the time.

Your Talents and Weaknesses

You bring great charm to many aspects of your life, including your career. You mix well, enjoying the company of others and wanting to make yourself agreeable to them.

You also have built-in taste that encourages you to

work in harmonious surroundings where your artistic fastidiousness can be used to good effect. You cannot bear dark, dirty conditions—nor, for that matter, dark, dirty co-workers.

You lack courage, resolution, and the power to make up your mind quickly. You will not take a tough risk, preferring the soft option.

Your strengths are your fair-mindedness, amiability and flair for colour, texture, and the use of conversation to get what you want.

Career Choices

In industry, in the personnel department, weights and measures department, finishing departments, in the rag trade and the manufacture of many fancy goods, luxury gifts, decorative goods.

In commerce, as receptionist, floor manager, public relations officer, florist and flower arranger, window dresser, shop assistant in fashion, conciliator.

In the social services, as social visitor.

In the arts, as graphic designer, photographer, fashion designer, theatre designer.

In the professions, in the Foreign Office as a diplomat.

17   COLD DEWS

Origins

Seventeenth of the 24 Chinese fortnightly periods covering the dates October 9th–23rd. Chinese name: *han lu*. Meaning: cold dews. Corresponds to the second half of the Zodiacal Sign of Libra.

Your Place in the World

As a youngster, you adopt a peaceful, love-thy-neighbour attitude towards the world. You like to be treated as one member of a wide circle of citizens organising their lives together with kindliness and amity.

As you grow older, however, you become more firm-minded in your political and social attitudes—even something of a fanatic. You want your political leaders to be strong men who can stand up to bullies and never give way in a crisis—all so different from your views in your younger days, when you want peace at almost any price.

Your Attitude to Work

It's the same story as far as your career is concerned. You start off in life in a faintly aimless fashion, trying your hand at a variety of jobs. It's only when you enter middle age that you're gripped by the need to specialise in a particular field of endeavour. Your overall aim in life is to be happy at work. Your means of obtaining happiness vary according to your age.

Your Talents and Weaknesses

You bring three splendid gifts to almost any work you tackle: personal charm, artistic merit and the ability to reach compromises. Clearly you need a job where these qualities are useful: dealing with other people, making them feel happy and at home, engaged in design-work of some sort or other, and helping to act as judge between warring parties.

Your weaknesses are equally obvious: a real lack of drive at times, a tendency to dither over important decisions, and the need to rely on someone else to assist you in making up your mind.

Clearly you suit 'civilised' conditions rather than the noise and dirt of the building site. Clearly, too, you need to work for, and with, other people. You aren't really suited for solitary labour, except artistic work.

Career Choices

In industry, in the staff welfare department, in manufacturing industries making furniture, fabrics, fashion, in the beauty industries (cosmetics especially).

In commerce, as hostess, public relations officer, worker

in beauty salon as hairdresser, manicurist, etc. Shop assistant, fashion buyer, negotiator on other people's behalf. *In the social services*, as marriage guidance counsellor, foster parent, work helping divorced people or women in distress.

In the arts, as almost anything, from model to designer, actor to writer. An emphasis on the visual arts.

In the professions, as divorce lawyer, international lawyer, landscape architect.

18   DESCENT OF HOAR FROST

Origins

Eighteenth of the 24 Chinese fortnightly periods covering the dates October 24th–November 7th. Chinese name: *shuang chiang*. Meaning: the descent of hoar frost. Corresponds to the first half of the Zodiacal Sign of Scorpio.

Your Place in the World

Each man must look after himself, in your estimation. The welfare state offends this belief in self-reliance, yet you are no anarchist. You see the need for firm government and get a kind of dramatic thrill from great international crises. A statesman, to gain your respect, must be a man of principle who is prepared to go it alone.

You adopt a similar position in your own role as citizen. You can be pushed around so far—but once the limit is reached, you prove obdurate to the point of bloody-mindedness.

Your Attitude to Work

Your ideal career is one in which you can channel all your pent-up energy and drive. You're a crusader, a person with an inner mission to fulfil. Unless—or until—you find this true mission in life, you can be inwardly unhappy, with a chip on your shoulder. Money, glory, the respect of the community—all these fade into insignificance compared with the overriding motivation: to be true to yourself.

Your Talents and Weaknesses

You work best in a career you believe in—one that gives you a large measure of responsibility and room for personal manoeuvre. You are a good organiser, and can make an excellent leader, especially of a closely-knit group of people with a crisis on their hands.

You respond magnificently to a challenge, and so should avoid the pussy-footing, timid sort of occupations where there's no competition and no opportunity to stretch yourself.

Your faults can be legion: a bolshie attitude towards a boss who doesn't suit you; an inflexibility of outlook, once your mind is made up; a difficulty in talking simply to people less intelligent than yourself (and a refusal to suffer fools gladly); and a lot of self-pity if people criticise you.

Career Choices

In industry, the tougher the better, anything from work on an oil rig to a job in heavy manufacturing industry. Anywhere up the scale of management.

In commerce, again as manager, especially in investment work. Specialised trades include butcher, undertaker, dry cleaner or launderer, debt collector and anti-pollution worker.

In the social services, as policeman or policewoman, especially detective work.

In the arts, as actor or actress, director of films.

In the professions, as criminal lawyer, engineer or research scientist (especially chemist).

Origins

Nineteenth of the 24 Chinese fortnightly periods covering the dates November 8th–22nd. Chinese name: *li tung*. Meaning: the beginning of Winter. Corresponds to the second half of the Zodiacal Sign of Scorpio.

Your Place in the World

You see yourself as someone who has to make your own way in life. You're as good as the next person, and certainly aren't a snob—yet at the same time, you can't easily accept help from others, and hate being beholden to them for past favours.

You may be left-wing or right-wing in your political views, but whatever attitudes you do hold will be held with conviction . . . to the point of obstinacy, at times. You are a person of principle, setting your own standards and not expecting other people to cooperate.

Your Attitude to Work

At work you can be single-minded, throwing yourself into a task with body and soul firing on all cylinders. But if the work doesn't suit you, you can equally be obstructive and unaccommodating. The most important motivation in life, as far as your career is concerned, is the need to feel the job itself is worthwhile and is somehow testing you to the limits of your capacity.

Your Talents and Weaknesses

You have fine concentration, excellent steadiness of nerve, plenty of courage in a tricky situation, and a tireless energy—so long as the work suits you. You make a good organiser, and though you don't grab attention in an immature way, you aren't desperately shy either.

But there are potential personality difficulties that can affect your work performance. Your instinctive need to be secretive means that you find it hard to be totally open and cooperative with colleagues. Your capacity to feel resentment long after the cause of the resentment has passed means that you can get emotional blocks, especially over the wrong kind of supervisor.

Career Choices

In industry, in civil and mechanical engineering work, especially tunnels; in construction work; in lonely, heavy industrial jobs where you carry the responsibility.

In commerce, as security officer, numerous forms of management work, shop walker, bank employee.

In the social services, as a mental health nurse.

In the arts, as satirist in words or graphics. Also as propagandist.

In the professions, as doctor or psychoanalyst, as a naval officer, as lawyer.

20   LESSER SNOW

Origins

Twentieth of the 24 Chinese fortnightly periods covering the dates November 23rd–December 7th. Chinese name: *hsiao hsueh*. Meaning: lesser snow. Corresponds to the first half of the Zodiacal Sign of Sagittarius.

Your Place in the World

You're an independent democrat, in the sense that you believe in all the democratic virtues—free speech, the right to partake in the process of government, the necessity of fair play in public life—but still like to go your own way, never allying yourself with the majority simply because it is the majority.

You like your statesmen to be honest, even slightly indiscreet men who live dangerously and are prepared to take risks to further their policies.

Your Attitude to Work

Nobody can call you a puritan who feels you *must* work for the good of your soul. Equally, you aren't a lazy person. Earning a living is simply a way of passing the time —and the more agreeably this can be done, the happier you'll be.

Money isn't as important as fame, but it has to be fame among people you respect. Fame isn't as important as freedom, by which you mean the ability to choose your own lifestyle and follow the career that suits your personality.

Your Talents and Weaknesses

Quite your most engaging quality is your ability to live by your wits. It's part resourcefulness, part lucky streak in your life that enables you to be the right person to meet the right opportunity at the right time.

You are fluent with words, agile with ideas. You can be highly persuasive, though there's a danger it will leave the realm of fact and descend into mere rhetoric.

Your weakness is lack of stamina. You find it temperamentally uncongenial to stick at a task through to its completion. This versatility has its advantages, to be sure —but can be a serious drawback. You need a job that gets you out and about, with a new problem on your mind every day. You loathe monotony and should avoid all jobs comprising a lot of routine labour.

Career Choices

In industry, building worker, steel erector, in electrical engineering, the biological sciences.

In commerce, in the export division, as a sales representative, as a trainer, dog-handler, athletic coach, somebody dealing with horses, public relations.

In the social services, in the Citizens' Advice Bureau.

In the arts, as a writer, broadcaster, publicist.

In the professions, in the Church or Law.

Origins

Twenty-first of the 24 Chinese fortnightly periods covering the dates December 8th–21st. Chinese name: *ta hsueh*. Meaning: the greater snow. Corresponds to the second half of the Zodiacal Sign of Sagittarius.

Your Place in the World

You see yourself as a person of independent views who wants to play a full, responsible role as a citizen. You are neither shyly introverted nor cocksurely boisterous, but certainly you have self-assurance allied to a proper modesty.

Two great qualities are needed in public affairs, to your way of thinking: vision and commonsense. You cannot abide statesmen with small parochial minds; nor can you see any point in political leaders lacking *nous*. They must be men of the world whose eyes are raised towards some noble aim.

Your Attitude to Work

You enjoy making an effort, and so the goal of personal achievement is perhaps the strongest motivation within your psyche. This is why you enjoy trying your hand at a variety of tasks in life; success in a new venture is more worthwhile than mere repetition of an old routine.

You also get a big kick from spreading enthusiasm to others. Ideally you treat work as a means of getting excited—and to transmit your excitement makes it even more valuable as an experience.

Your Talents and Weaknesses

Your skills lie in your questing mind, that loves making fresh discoveries and building up a store of knowledge that you can communicate to others; and in your qualities of leadership that seem able to get other people to o-operate because they want to.

Your faults are too versatile an approach, so that you are sometimes not single-minded enough; and an occasional slipshod method of working that can make silly mistakes through carelessness rather than real stupidity. You should avoid routine precision work, and look for those jobs that seem to offer some degree of adventure.

You can be skilful in your hands, and a certain amount of bodily movement is necessary in an ideal job.

Career Choices

In industry, as driver, crane operator, pilot, railman; as nuclear engineer, technologist in welding, materials testing, petroleum products.

In commerce, as translator, interpreter; as travel guide; as solicitors' clerk, stock exchange jobber, journalist; as teleprint operator.

In the social services, as fireman or ambulance worker; as a legal aid adviser.

In the arts, as playwright, circus performer.

In the professions, as a lecturer (especially in languages, international affairs, science and philosophy).

22   WINTER SOLSTICE

Origins

Twenty-second of the 24 Chinese fortnightly periods covering the dates December 22nd–January 5th. Chinese name: *tung chih*. Meaning: the Winter solstice. Corresponds to the first half of the Zodiacal Sign of Capricorn.

Your Place in the World

Your aim in life is to get a good grip on reality. You're a practical, hard-working, serious-minded individual who wants to be a model citizen: obedient, thrifty, friendly towards the neighbours but sticking to the good old standards in life.

Inevitably you edge towards the right-wing in politics, for you admire the Establishment and respect the traditional way of life. You like your statesmen to be efficient, orderly men with a wealth of experience behind them. You are not much impressed by youth.

Your Attitude to Work

This ambitious approach to life is reflected in your attitude towards your career. You take it extremely seriously, and couldn't slip from one occupation to the next just like that; you take a long-term view of where you're going, and how you'll get there. All the 'sensible' goals motivate you: money, security, respectable fame, and pride in your own achievements. You even want to help other people — for their own good!

Your Talents and Weaknesses

You bring all the orderly virtues to work with you: efficiency, punctuality, fine ability to organise and administer, a cool logical mind relatively unswayed by sentiment and, not least, the capacity to keep other employees up to scratch, if not through inspired leadership at least through putting the fear of God into them.

Your weaknesses stem from these virtues. At times you treat other people as mere rungs in your own ladder of advancement, automata who should do as they're told. You have much patience with human failings, in short, including your own.

Your mind can be inflexible, though a well-argued case will change it more than a sloppy appeal to the heart. You are excellent at precision-work, but not very inventive. Once you've learnt a principle, you tend to apply it whatever the circumstances.

Career Choices

In industry, almost anywhere, though you'll certainly want to rise through the ranks some way up the hierarchy: foreman, supervisor right up to managing director. You really are best suited to manufacturing industries where there's a solid end-product.

In commerce, as accountant, financial analyst, administrator, from efficient secretary to chairman of the company.

In the social services, as a behind-the-scenes organiser in local authority or Civil Service: the person making decisions, carrying the can, getting the practical details right.

In the arts, as architect.

In the professions, as clergyman, teacher of mathematics or history.

23   LESSER COLD

Origins

Twenty-third of the 24 Chinese fortnightly periods covering the dates January 6th–20th. Chinese name: *hsiao han*. Meaning: the lesser cold. Corresponds to the second half of the Zodiacal Sign of Capricorn.

Your Place in the World

You're an intensely community-minded individual, caring strongly for public affairs, current events, politics and the way your local neighbourhood is run. You see yourself helping to run the show—not for glory so much as the simple pleasure of holding the reins of power, in however small a way.

You respect experience more than any other attribute —experience you have gained yourself or acquired second-hand through study of books. You like a well-ordered society where nobody misbehaves or departs too much from the norms. You honour older people, and like your political leaders to be honest, tactful men working more behind the scenes than in full public glare.

Your Attitude to Work

Work is like food to you; you need a certain amount every day simply to keep alive. You see it as a duty, as a way of providing for your crochety old age, as the only possible activity between nine and five during fifty weeks of the year. But in reality you are hooked on it, like a drug addict. You adore work, including the long boring bits. You wake up secretly exhilarated at the thought of trudging to the office or factory.

Your Talents and Weaknesses

You are quite capable of working for a large institution or company, for you enjoy being one ant out of many with alloted tasks to be finished as efficiently as possible.

You are an admirable compromiser, excellent at committee work and encouraging co-workers to play their part in the wonderful drama of Bloggs International Inc. People, in turn, admire your dedication and loyalty, your marvellous perseverance in the face of difficulties, your attention to detail . . . even your caution when called for.

They may not admire so much the coldness with which you can occasionally treat other people, the depressive anxieties that could lead to an early ulcer, the lack of adaptability in outlook that characterises your working life from middle age onwards.

Career Choices

In industry, as inspector, production manager, work in maintenance, shop steward, construction worker.

In commerce, as computer programmer, punch-card operator, machinist, banker, civil service official.

In the social services, as geriatric nurse, work with senior citizens' welfare.

In the arts, as musician or composer, a revivialist of earlier fashions.

In the professions, as headmaster, professor or research worker in an academic discipline; possibly as a soldier.

24   GREATER COLD

Origins

Twenty-fourth of the 24 Chinese fortnightly periods covering the dates January 21st–February 4th. Chinese name: *ta han.* Meaning: the greater cold. Corresponds to the first half of the Zodiacal Sign of Aquarius.

Your Place in the World

You see yourself as a citizen of the whole world—not one little country with limited national horizons but the total brotherhood of man. You hate pettiness of any description; you love to think big, paint a broad canvas, see things on a large scale. And you expect your ideal political leaders to do the same: to avoid mean arguments, to get round age-old obstacles, to have the vision and will to create a new society.

In your everyday life, you are prepared to play your role, for you are as equal to the task as the next man or woman. You embrace worthwhile causes, and create a climate of change in your neighbourhood.

Your Attitude to Work

You need to feel that any career you follow has a purpose over and above earning you a living. It must have social value, in however small a way. What you really enjoy is a crusade, especially against the enemies of poverty, ignorance and bureaucratic red tape.

Your Talents and Weaknesses

You bring some excellent qualities to whatever work you do: great fairness towards others coupled with a belief in their humanity, which must come before mere businesslike efficiency; a keen mind with quite an inventive, ingenious streak that enables you to see a new solution to an old problem; and excellent powers of observation that encourage you to draw sensible conclusions from a mass of facts at your disposal.

Your weaknesses are a slight lack of drive, especially at the decision-making level, and a refusal to use your personality to further your aims.

You are suited to an institutional way of life so long as you don't feel imprisoned by routine or cramped by lack of personal initiative. You can function very well as a self-employed person, though you may need a partner to help you make fast, hard decisions.

Career Choices

In industry, as electrician, industrial photographer, glass-worker, diamond-cutter, technologist in numerous fields.

In commerce, as shop assistant in electronics, fashion, health foods; as air steward or ground crew with an airline; telephonist or Telex operator. As journalist, printer, publisher.

In the social services, as blood transfusion worker, radiologist, any therapist using electrical equipment; as a teacher of science especially.

In the arts, as a worker in the movies or television.

In the professions, as psychologist, academic in an erudite, mildly obscure subject; as a science fiction writer.

THE FOURTH PATH—Your Day of Birth

Introduction

The next stage—the most complex and in some ways most personal—in understanding your character is based on the precise day, month and year of birth.

This Fourth Path is concerned with the 28 Chinese *hsui* or lunar mansions, as they are sometimes called, despite the fact that the moon may never pass through some of them. Early Chinese astronomy was built around certain circumpolar stars—that is, stars that were always above the horizon in China at that time. By drawing an imaginative line through each of these determinative stars and the equatorial pole (the same as our own Pole Star today) they created a grid that enabled them to know the exact locations of all other stars, including the Sun and Moon, even if they appeared to be way below the horizon at the time.

If you picture various segments of an orange radiating from the pole, then those segments meet the middle of the orange (the celestial equator) are the 28 *hsui*.

There are various problems in trying to fit this ancient method of criss-crossing the sky into our modern ideas of astrology and the interpretation of character. Since these *hsui* or asterisms were devised, probably back in the 14th century B.C., the sky has changed a good deal. Some stars have got brighter, others dimmer; some have moved out of one constellation into another; and most important of all, the precession of the equinoxes has changed the relationship between the Sun's path and the celestial equator on which these asterisms are based. Certain stars which were circumpolar have ceased to be. Thus Kio, the first of the 24 Chinese asterisms, now is situated around the middle of the Tropical Sign of Libra, whereas back in say 2400 B.C. it lay at the end of Leo.

The upshot is that I have done the same for this circle of *hsui* as modern astrologers have done for the Zodiac. Once upon a time, about the time of Christ, there was a single Zodiac based on the actual stars grouped into constellations in the sky. Nowadays this so-called Sidereal Zodiac is still used, mainly in the East; but Western astrologers follow the Tropical Zodiac, which is man-made and fractionally, year by year, inches away from the old Sidereal one. All the Signs in the new Zodiac are the same size; but the trouble with the old system is that the constellations are all different shapes and sizes, and nobody really knows where one of them ends and the next one begins.

It's the same with these Chinese *hsui*. They all vary in size, and we don't know whether their size today bears any resemblance to their size a couple of millenia ago. So I've equalled them up, made the circle start at roughly the same right ascension each year, and hoped for the best!

The other problem has lain in what each *hsui* means. If you go back to the *Shih Chi* of Ssuma Chhien, about 100 B.C., you find predictions like: —

If the fire-planet Mars forces its way into the *hsui* Kio, then there will be fighting. If it is in the *hsui* Fang or Hsin, this will be hateful to kings.

This is hardly helpful to us today, when there is always fighting somewhere in the world and when kings, presidents and prime ministers are universally hated by their electorates!

The personality descriptions given here are a mixture of Chinese sources, a look at the somewhat similar Indian and Babylonian lunar mansions, and some first-hand experience in observing people with the moon in particular *hsui*.

What You Have To Do

Add the year number (from Table 1 below) to the month number (from Table 2), to correspond with the year and month of your birth. Then add the actual date of your birth. If the answer is more than 28, subtract 28. (If it's *still* more than 28, subtract another 28.) The result is your Asterism number, and from Table 3 you can see where to read the characteristics of your particular *hsui*. Remember that the description given applies to only one part of your total personality: your emotional disposition, the way you inwardly react to life—and to other people—and in particular your love life.

If you feel your chosen asterism is quite wrong for you, it's possible that one of the asterisms on either side is the right one for you. But don't swop and change simply to avoid facing an unpleasant truth about yourself! The majority of you will be correctly calculated.

Example: Paul McCartney, born June 18th 1942

His Animal Asterism

	18	(from Table 1, for 1942)
	13	(from Table 2, for June)
	18	(for 18th day)
	49	
take away	28	
	21	which is Ape

Example: Prince Charles, born November 14th, 1948

His Animal Asterism

	24	(from Table 1, for 1948)
	24	(from Table 2, for November)
	14	(for 14th day)
	62	
take away	28	
	34	
Take away another	28	
	6	which is Tiger

129

TABLE 1
The Year Numbers 1880–1980

Year	Year No	Year	Year No	Year	Year No
1880	24	1913	27	1946	4
1881	6	1914	9	1947	14
1882	16	1915	21	1948	24
1883	27	1916	3	1949	7
1884	10	1917	13	1950	17
1885	20	1918	24	1951	27
1886	2	1919	6	1952	9
1887	12	1920	16	1953	21
1888	23	1921	26	1954	3
1889	5	1922	8	1955	13
1890	15	1923	17	1956	24
1891	25	1924	1	1957	6
1892	7	1925	11	1958	15
1893	17	1926	22	1959	26
1894	27	1927	4	1960	9
1895	9	1928	15	1961	18
1896	21	1929	25	1962	0
1897	3	1930	7	1963	11
1898	13	1931	17	1964	23
1899	24	1932	27	1965	4
1900	6	1933	9	1966	14
1901	15	1934	21	1967	24
1902	26	1935	3	1968	7
1903	9	1936	13	1969	17
1904	18	1937	24	1970	27
1905	0	1938	6	1971	9
1906	11	1939	15	1972	21
1907	23	1940	26	1973	3
1908	4	1941	9	1974	13
1909	15	1942	18	1975	24
1910	25	1943	0	1976	6

Year	Year No		Year	Year No		Year	Year No
1911	7		1944	11		1977	15
1912	17		1945	23		1978	26
						1979	8

TABLE 2
The Month Numbers

MONTH	MONTH NO
January	0
February	24
March	22
April	20
May	17
June	13
July	9
August	6
September	3
October	0
November	24
December	22

TABLE 3
The Animal Asterisms

No	1	HORNLESS DRAGON	See page 132
No	2	DRAGON	See page 134
No	3	BADGER	See page 136
No	4	HARE	See page 138
No	5	FOX	See page 140
No	6	TIGER	See page 142
No	7	LEOPARD	See page 144
No	8	GRYPHON	See page 146
No	9	OX	See page 149
No	10	BAT	See page 151
No	11	RAT	See page 153
No	12	SWALLOW	See page 155

HORNLESS DRAGON   1

Origin

First of the 28 Chinese asterisms, situated in the Eastern
Palace. Chinese name: *chio*. Original meaning: the horn.
Position: 12° in extent, starting at α Virginis. Includes
Spica.

Your Emotional Nature

A lively, friendly disposition with a lot of time for
other people and an interest in their affairs. You find it
pretty easy to stay optimistic, partly because you have a
cheerful response to life and partly because you are inquisitive about the future.

Certainly your typical reaction to life is to say 'Yes',
even though your better judgment would urge you to
reply 'No' or 'Maybe'. There's a dash of foolhardiness in
your feelings; they well up out of your subconscious, spill-
ing over into your everyday life without a great deal of
control. You like to get your feelings out into the open—

and once they're out, you almost forget about them. This is why people may go on feeling a grudge against something you've said or done, long after you yourself have forgotten the incident. This is why you can sometimes seem indiscreet, tactless and downright insensitive to the feelings of others. You're too self-centred.

Self-centred, remember, isn't the same as selfish or greedy, though at worst it can become that. It simply means that everything that you perceive has to be filtered through your own attitudes, preconceptions and prejudices; everything you do has to be an expression of your own desires, even though the desire may be selfless duty to others. The cynical saying that 'Charity is only enlightened self-interest' seems to apply to you more than many people.

Your best points, as far as your emotional nature is concerned, are your splendid courage to say what you think is right, your determination to stand up and be counted, your self-confidence and ability to handle other people with ease. Above all, you can at best convey enthusiasm to the people around you. You can charge them with your own special brand of psychic electricity and set them tingling with zest and appetite for life.

Your worst points are your emotional brashness and occasional lack of sympathy with people's real feelings; you're often too concerned with expressing how you feel to worry about your effect on others. You can sometimes seem crude to the sensitive folk of this world.

The Hornless Dragon Male

If you're a man, all the upstanding, masculine characteristics of this animal asterism will be expressed easily enough through your sexuality. You may be a bit too much of a good thing, and will need a bit of grace and charm elsewhere in your Chinese horoscope to counteract this rather dominant, cheerful Charlie persona. You'll function well in men's clubs, stag parties, etc; less happily in afternoon tea-sessions with the ladies.

The Hornless Dragon Woman

The female of the species has a kind of rude health about her. You're pleased with yourself, a bit of a tomboy as a girl, maybe something of a man-eater as an adult. You need a strong man as a partner (weak ones you gobble up in no time) but inevitably there's going to be a clash of wills. Fortunately your good humour sees you through many difficulties, but every so often your air of competitiveness refuses to let you compromise.

Love and Sex

Most Hornless Dragons have a high-voltage sexuality, though it can become divorced from the deeper emotions of love, loyalty and respect. If you take time to appreciate the needs of your partner, you can make a wonderful lover. Certainly there's always liable to be an element of romantic surprise where you're concerned. Suddenly, out of the blue, you'll rush home with an expensive bunch of flowers—or, if you're the woman, you'll have a marvellous dinner by candlelight waiting for the tired husband back from work.

DRAGON 2

Origin

Second of the 28 Chinese asterisms, situated in the Eastern Palace. Chinese name: *khang*. Original meaning: neck. Position: 9° in extent, starting at κ Virginis.

Your Emotional Nature

In many ways you're similar to the Hornless Dragon: vigorous, hearty, inclined to take the lead early even if you haven't the stamina to win a long-distance race. You're essentially a sprint runner, dashing into the fray, pausing for breath, and then onward into some new venture.

Your typical emotional response to life is brave, open-hearted and even a little childlike. You aren't the cynical city type; by temperament you're the out-of-doors sort. You need to be on the move—from one job to another, one home to the next, even one friend after another.

Where you differ from the Hornless Dragon type is in your approach to leadership. Hornless loves to take command of a situation, but hasn't your inner flair that encourages others to respect you as a leader. He puffs and snorts in an effort to grab attention. You, at your best, seem able to capture it without nearly so much effort.

You should love sports and games of all descriptions, especially those involving a real challenge. There's a racy quality to so much that you think and do—even your handwriting is likely to be dashed off with plenty of verve but little attention to detail. This is your trouble: too much enthusiasm, not sufficient care and consideration. Other folk, particularly asterisms Ox, Raven and Tapir, will find you annoyingly inaccurate, slapdash and unpunctual. Not because you're vague—just that you pack so much into your day that you can't afford the time to fuss about itsy-bitsy trivia.

Your best points are your warm-hearted friendliness and loyalty, though of course there's a tinge of self-centredness that makes it hard for you to appreciate the depth and subtlety of other people's emotions.

Your worst points are your occasional tantrums, your tendency to get impatient and vent your anger on innocent bystanders, and sometimes your overbearing manner. If other parts of your Chinese horoscope are more dithery than this Dragon piece, you'll feel like overcompensating and really throwing your weight around without a great deal of confidence.

The Dragon Male

If you're a man, the strength and vitality of this animal asterism will be apparent to all. You'll get on well with all kinds of people, but you're essentially a man's man who enjoys boisterous male company. With women you can get over-familiar too quickly—or, equally bad, ignore them if they don't meet your standards.

The Dragon Woman

There's a touch of the shrew in your nature. Certainly you enjoy wearing the trousers and, like Annie, like to think you can equal any man in his achievements. At best you're a champion of women's rights, or a highly capable organiser of women's clubs. Certainly you can run a business—or a family—with gusto and efficiency.

Love and Sex

Your strong libido means that there's a sexual element in nearly all your relationships. It adds tang and bite. You'll succeed in love where you manage to make your appeal less blatant. It's as though you feel you have to ooze sex appeal, whereas in fact it's perfectly obvious to everyone that you're a sensual individual. So relax!

BADGER 3

Origin

Third of the 28 Chinese asterisms, situated in the Eastern Palace. Chinese name: *ti*. Original meaning: the root. Position: 15° in extent, starting at α Librae.

Your Emotional Nature

Essentially you're the loyal, plodding steady type with lots of innate tolerance and good humour. There's something of the traditional British bobby about you: everyone's friend (except the real villains) but refusing to make a favourite of anyone.

Think of the badger in nature, slowly meandering along familiar paths in the forest, never moving far from his set, a bit shy, certainly not flaunting himself in the open light of day. Well, that's a fair analogy of your own emotional response to life. You like the well-known routine of your everyday life, and, particularly as you get older, dislike being torn from your nice, worn habits. You aren't a show-off, but equally you haven't an inferiority complex: you like to stand four-square in the world, confident of yourself but not needing to prove it to other folk.

This third animal asterism originally meant 'the root', which exactly sums up your typical instinct in life. With friends, you want to put down real, lasting roots of affection; you aren't the hail-fellow-well-met chap who can skip from friendship to friendship without any responsibility. Your friends are for life. You'll stand by them, even in crises, and you expect the same from them.

The settled, domestic lifestyle suits you. Probably you love collecting things, hoarding old personal belongings and, equally as important, hoarding memories of old loves . . . and, unfortunately, old hates, too. This is a disagreeable trait with all you Badger types: your tendency to seethe inwardly with feelings of revenge long after the wrong was originally committed.

The Badger Male

You suit most gatherings except the very artificial jet-set type of society. You aren't good with ironic people, either; you take their clever jokes too seriously. In women you admire the real Earth Goddess qualities of honesty, good looks of a statuesque kind, a warm air of motherhood and a sense of companionship that's ideal for a long life of marriage together.

The Badger Woman

You aren't too comfortable with obviously intelligent people, because you're mainly instinctual yourself, operating more through your heart than your head. You look for a strong, reliable man; you put faithfulness high on your list of desirable qualities in a prospective husband. Despite your firmness of mind, once you've made it up, you still expect the man to take the important decisions in life, and you look to him for leadership and enthusiasm.

Love and Sex

Badgers are highly sexed, but it takes a long time for you to attain the necessary plateau of familiarity before you're prepared to release the full volume of your sexual response. Avoid two-faced, tricky, here-today-and-off-tomorrow partners. As a general rule, keep to your own kind: you don't mix with 'alien' people awfully well.

HARE 4

Origins

Fourth of the 28 Chinese asterisms, situated in the Eastern Palace. Chinese name: *fang*. Original meaning: the room. Position: 5° in extent, starting at π Scorpii.

Your Emotional Nature

Quick-witted, amusing, loving to move on to a brand-new experience, endlessly inquisitive and yet unreliable to a fault—that's the summation of your emotional response to life. People find you enormous fun—for a while. Then you can seem too full of yourself, too vain, too eager to present yourself in an attractive light.

Often you seem to have the manner of the persuasive salesman, keen to win the argument whether or not you have justice or truth on your side. The intricacies of debate appeal to you. You're the kind of person, in fact, who is drawn to clever, abstract games like chess, crossword puzzles and word quizzes.

Individuals as widely ranging as philosophers and wise-cracking comedians can be Hares: the thing you all have in common is a delight in the wiles and guiles of the human mind and an interest in impressing others with the brilliance and speed of your own brain.

In your social life, you are tremendously gregarious, loving to mix with people of all sorts and conditions. It's comparatively difficult for you to settle down with one person to form a deep intimate relationship. You need a partner who'll respond to the many facets of your emotional disposition—and somebody with the good-natured tolerance to put up with your zany moods.

In the last moral resort, you aren't the person of great principle. If things get too tough, if you can no longer wriggle out of a situation and run away, then you're inclined to break down in a childish tantrum, or, if you're really frightened, in a fawning, please-forgive-me stance.

At best, therefore, you are versatile, ingenious and a bundle of intriguing ideas. At worst, you are slipshod and ultimately caught up in pleasure at the sight of your own reflection.

The Hare Male

You enjoy chatting up the birds—so much so, in fact, that even after you're happily married you'll keep up one or two flirtations, just to keep your hand in. It's tempting for you to treat love-making as the Frenchman is traditionally meant to do: as a necessary and delightful form of physical and emotional hygiene. You haven't really the richness of feeling for the Grand Passion.

The Hare Woman

Your nature changes a lot once you've a home and family to run. Settled domestic life doesn't really suit you, and unless you can find the opportunity to be sociable in clubs and associations and coffee mornings, you'll get riled at your circumstances and fundamentally frustrated. You need a husband who can provide security without asking you to work towards it: in other words, leaving you free to get on with the amusing things in life.

Love and Sex

Both men and women of the Hare pack can be marvellously affectionate creatures, adept in the ways of love and treating it as a clever conversation ... and the best conversations never end, do they? Your faults are perhaps an impatience with the fussy, fastidious partner—and, in the last resort, a failure to be able to put yourself totally in the heart of another.

FOX 5

Origins

Fifth of the 28 Chinese asterisms, situated in the Eastern Palace. Chinese name: *hsin*. Original meaning: the heart. Position: 5° in extent, starting at σ Scorpii. Includes Antares.

Your Emotional Nature

Essentially you're a warm-hearted, generous individual with a liking for life that comes through in your delight in open-air pursuits, your feeling for Nature and a desire to make the most of the time available to you.

But just as the fox is a much-misunderstood animal, so can your own emotional responses be taken the wrong way by other people. They can mistake your warmth for some kind of greed, your generosity for a subtle way of inveigling yourself into someone's good books. As a result, you'll have developed from childhood on an instinctive wariness about other people, and a tendency to make extra-sure that they understand how honest and open and above-board you really are.

Sometimes you may seem to protest too much, laboriously explaining your feelings—especially to members of the other sex!—so much that they may suspect that underneath all that verbiage you really are a pretty tricky customer. But by now you should be used to people failing to appreciate your inner virtues, so you may have developed the typical Foxy attitude of a rueful shrug and a smile.

The truth is that, although you seem affable to most people, the real You only shows itself in long-lasting close relationships—in the family circle, in your place of work perhaps, with a handful of old friends. But even with them, there's a tendency for you to change your personality to suit the conditions of the moment. You don't really enjoy hurting others, but inwardly fear that they may think you do—so, to compensate for this, you go out of your way to make yourself pleasant and fit in with their plans and outlook, opinions and prejudices.

Although you're not the moody, broody type, you have moments of introspection when you need to reflect upon your own nature and its impact on others. Quite a few novelists and psychologists are Fox people, for instance, and teachers also feature among typical Fox professions.

Your best points are your combination of simplicity and complexity, the way you can devise an overall plan of campaign and fill in the details as well. Well-meaning and sensitive, you have much to offer the world.

At worst, however, you can develop an inferiority attitude which you might cover up with a show of good-natured bluster.

The Fox Male

You have a strong virility ideally combined with a sensitivity towards women—your chances of becoming a mature, well-rounded husband and lover are therefore excellent. Equally, however, the two sides to your emotional nature can conflict, leading to anxiety about your effectiveness in these roles. You are particularly concerned with the way women take you. At best, it seems you're a real ladies' man. At worst, a man unsure of yourself.

The Fox Female

As a Vixen you are both hunter and protector, career woman and housewife. In your relationships with men, you like to make the running—but, contrariwise, need to feel you are being chased as well! As with males of the species, you can either be a fine, well-balanced individual —or, if other factors in your Chinese horoscope are in conflict, a rather unhappy, at-odds-with-yourself person.

Love and Sex

Enough has been said to indicate that Fox types have a rich emotional response ideally suited to married life. You are too sensitive for a free-and-easy sex life outside marriage—but if a marriage went seriously wrong, you could establish a second permanent liaison as a kind of substitute marriage.

TIGER   6

Origins

Sixth of the 28 Chinese asterisms, situated in the Eastern Palace. Chinese name: *wei*. Original meaning: the tail. Position: 18° in extent, starting at μ Scorpii.

Your Emotional Nature

Instinctively people will sense that you are a powerfully endowed human being, as far as feelings are concerned. Life affects you at a gut level. You develop strong, black-or-white emotions that seem to grip you, though they needn't linger so much that they become obsessions.

In short, you have a splendid animal magnetism that gives you clear likes and dislikes—about people, about places, about ideas of all sorts. Combined with this is your charm, a hearty and optimistic kind that makes you quickly attractive to some people and equally annoying to others. When this charm of yours is unforced, it's a delightful quality in your demeanour. Only when it's laid on with a trowel will some people feel that you're more than they can bear.

Because you're a powerful character in the way you react to life, you may not always appreciate the strength of people's opposition to you—nobody, after all, wants to show too much open hostility to a Tiger! So you may breeze along in your merry way, little realising that a friend or relative is slowly building up a store of resentment that may abruptly explode, one day, shattering your blithe self-confidence.

As you work through your heart, not your head, it's hard to argue with you. At worst, you can be an ignorant bigot in certain matters, an Alf Garnett or Archie Bunker. At best, your flair for sensing the all-important subconscious undercurrents in human affairs lets you get to the nub of a situation straightaway, holding fast to that truth until the rest of the world catches up with you.

So much in your lifestyle depends on flair. Any sportsman knows when the magic is working his way; body and mind neatly dovetail so that he doesn't have to calculate what he must do—he simply does it, effortlessly. You, more than most of us, have access to a similar magic in your everyday disposition. It's great while it lasts—but on those bad days when it's lacking, you find life extra-hard, like wading through water.

People appreciate your courage, good humour and practicality. But they'll probably dislike your occasional bouts of bombast and your lack of concern for things that don't interest you.

The Tiger Male

It's natural for you to take command of a situation, which is needed in many man–woman relationships, but you have a tendency to keep the little lady in her place which is unfashionable in these days of Women's Lib and, at worst, downright tyrannical. It's the woman with a lot of character herself who brings out the best in you. The precious butterfly type of woman does nothing but encourage you to stick her in your collection.

The Tiger Woman

Miss Tigress can be a formidably alluring creature, radiant with sex appeal and none too cautious what she does with it. She can also be a spiteful, disdainful animal when hurt, and a real sour-puss when neglected.

Madame Tiger can also develop a sad, catty manner, if she's abandoned by her mate or ignored by him. She needs to live in a constant aura of affection—from her family, her husband . . . oh yes, and a little innocent attention from the milkman, too!

Love and Sex

You need love as a vital fuel. Perhaps your fault is to demand more than you are prepared to give, though you'll hate to be told this! You shouldn't allow any other more inhibiting factor in your Chinese horoscope to spoil the fulfilment of this marvellous sensual equipment of yours.

LEOPARD 7

Origins

Seventh of the 28 Chinese asterisms, situated in the Eastern Palace. Chinese name: *chi*. Original meaning: the winnowing basket, for separating the grain from the chaff. Position: 11° in extent, starting at γ Sagittarii.

Your Emotional Nature

Imagine the following characters: a foppish actor, a fastidious man of letters, a capable but not-always-popular lady chairman of a committee, a stand-offish head waiter at a grand restaurant. Put them all together, and you have an impression of the way you strike other people in some of your mannerisms. It's an unfair method of describing your emotional disposition . . . but as true as any caricature.

As you know, you have a vain disposition. A nicer way of putting it would be to say that you have self-respect, know your own virtues and won't indulge in false modesty. But don't think that vanity corresponds with boastfulness. You tend to hold your self-love in, privately admiring yourself whilst presenting a demure, cultivated facade.

Hopefully, life has taught you how to moderate this conceit so that it's merely a pleasant self-assurance. But there's liable to be an everpresent tendency to drop into a cynical attitude, simply to boost your own ego. Characters played by those fine movie actors George Sanders and Dennis Price often betray this civilised-snide Leopard facade.

So much for your faults. The best side of your typical response to life is your crisp intellectual grasp of the essentials of a situation. Your mind is quick yet shrewd, not particularly optimistic but rarely falling into the disreputable habit of depression. Your humour is ironic, dry, and rarely told against yourself. Your courage is a front, behind which you may be twitching with anxiety.

It follows that you don't find it easy to give yourself to others as openly—even naively—as you would sometimes wish. This sarky, artificial side to you intrudes on a sentimental occasion. At times you may hate yourself for being so fussy . . . but the truth is that you cannot help showing your snobbery.

The Leopard Male

You need the props of the gentleman—wealth, nice manners, maybe some good family connections in the background—to reassure you that you can manage women the way you want. Without them, the act seems a bit tatty. The genuinely mature Leopard has great suavity and consideration for others; the immature type is always trying to impress people with how much *savoire-faire* he has. You must learn to be brave enough to be sincere about your real feelings.

The Leopard Woman

At your best, there's a slinky grace to your beauty that must capture many male hearts—at a distance. Whether they like you so much at close quarters depends on whether you have faith in yourself as an ordinary, common-or-garden woman. If you stop giving yourself airs, if you're prepared to be pleasant to people whatever their circumstances in life, then you can develop a warmth and easy-going softness that will enhance any marriage. The older Leopard woman, particularly the frustrated kind, feels she needs to stand on her dignity.

Love and Sex

Because a subtler variety of feelings run through your psyche than the blood-and-thunder kind, you treat love as a clever game rather than a deathless passion. You need a partner who will act as an appropriate foil to your wit. It's the people with plenty of innate tolerance, like No 3 Badger, No 9 Ox, No 14 Porcupine who are the right sounding board; other types, closer to your own nature, such as No 10 Bat, No 19 Raven and No 22 Tapir, are compatible.

GRYPHON   8

Origins

Eighth of the 28 Chinese asterisms, situated in the Northern Palace. Chinese name: *nan tou*. Original meaning: the southern Dipper. Position: 26° in extent, starting at φ Sagittarii.

Your Emotional Nature

You adopt a keen-witted, independent attitude to life so that you can take nothing—and nobody—for granted.

By the same token, you allow no one to take you for granted, either; you enjoy being a bit of an individualist, and if things start getting dull, you stir them up with an outrageous remark, an unexpected piece of behaviour.

You take pleasure in going out on a limb, especially in adopting unorthodox ideas and defending them against more conventional minds. At worst, this can become mere devilment, discomforting people with less agile minds than your own.

At best, however, you can move straight to the heart of a problem, solving it with an ingenious answer that goes beyond logic into the realms of intuition.

You're a sociable person—with a difference! You like to mix with people, but need to stand out from the crowd, not because you're an exhibitionist but due to your inner desire to consider yourself an individualist. At times this will make you seem aloof, like a spectator of a football match instead of an actual player, but you certainly aren't snobbish—indeed, you'll go out of your way to befriend people a bit out of the ordinary, especially if they're another race or religion or political creed.

Most Gryphons have the sense of humour and inner poise to enjoy being ' a character'. This is tremendously true as Gryphons get older—they love sitting on park benches amiably saying oddball things to passers-by, or being known in the local Senior Citizens' group as a lovable scamp.

But some of your number, mainly in the teenage years when it's so important to conform to the standards of your own contemporaries, feel self-conscious about their emotional urge to react differently and unpredictably from their fellows. This can lead to the introverted Gryphon, a clever researcher into many little alley-ways of knowledge such as folklore, magic, fossils, herbal medicine and the like. By middle age he's built up a fund of fascinating, useless information. He attends quaint learned societies, or can be seen rummaging the country-side for a rare specimen of something or other.

As a Gryphon, you have barely a shred of cruelty in your nature. By and large, you're a kindly, canny, mildly rum sort of person. Most other persons start by wanting to smile at your foibles. As they get to know you better, they learn to smile *with* you.

The Gryphon Male

Some women find you too tame, others too wrapped up in your own interests. It's true that you don't easily flatter women, nor are you a primarily virile chap needing to prove his virility all the time. It's true, too, that you don't welcome intimate liaisons with open arms. They have to grow on you, sideways so to speak, so that you drift into cosy familiarity. You make an excellent husband provided your wife allows you plenty of freedom. (You need a study, a large garden and plenty of out-houses where you can pursue your multifarious hobbies in peace.)

The Gryphon Woman

You get on better with men than with your own sex, though once women have grown used to your funny little ways they learn to appreciate your sterling qualities beneath. You tend to see men as intriguing boys who need washing, feeding and plenty of exercise. (Some Gryphon women establish marvellous relationships with animals on the same basis.) You don't flaunt yourself as a sex object, but need to capture a man's imagination. You are quite good running a weak man's life for him. Certainly you should avoid the tough, bullying type.

Love and Sex

All Gryphons tend to see the sex drive as part of the eternal Life Force rather than a means to parenthood or even temporary pleasure. At best, you're capable of marvellously enduring love relationships, composed more of companionship than sexual desire. At worst, there's a touch of the eccentric bachelor or spinster about you—

and even in marriage you need some privacy from your partner.

OX   9

Origins

Ninth of the 28 Chinese asterisms, situated in the Northern Palace. Chinese name: *niu* or *chhien niu*. Original meaning: an ox or herd boy. Position: 8° in extent, starting at β Capricorni.

Your Emotional Nature

The Ox is a steady, strong, patient and persevering animal working six days a week and, as he's been told to do, resting on the seventh by lolling in a meadow doing nothing but chew the cud. And in so many ways you're just the same! You've the same constructive zeal, the same conservatism of outlook, the identical good-natured tolerance and stamina. Above all, after all the energy you have thrown into life, you need the same time to flop into a deck-chair and be served the creature comforts of food and drink by someone else for a change.

You adopt a realistic, practical and down-to-earth approach to life, and your emotional responses often betray this materialistic understanding. You like to bring arguments down to concrete, black-and-white points; you tend to debunk the high-falutin', airy-fairy type of sentiments. Your brand of humour is the solid belly laugh, and whether or not you admit it to others, you enjoy a dirty joke or two!

Your faults are obvious to everyone, even yourself. You aren't adventurous enough, so that you get stuck in your own habits just as your increasing girth as you get older will get you stuck in your favourite arm-chair. Your ideas veer towards the traditional for the sake of tradition. Your feelings get rooted in the same old groove so that it's impossible to budge you from preconceptions and prejudices.

In short, you're inflexible—and while you may call this a stand on a matter of principle, other people say it's just old Ox being obstinately bloody-minded!

They'll tend to call you 'old so-and-so' from quite a young age, simply because you exude an air of steady responsibility from the word go. People come to you for advice; they trust your dependable manner; they know you will keep your promise and honour your commitments. This weight—or *gravitas* as it used to be called—is your most precious asset and most enduring characteristic.

The Ox Male

You're the ideal family man, made for marriage to a good woman and the role of father to a brood of fine children. Promiscuity offends your innate approach to life—and besides, you aren't very good at it, for you cannot tell lies easily, nor are you a natural flirter. Your view of the male–female relationship is an old-fashioned one, with the man as the provider and the woman as nurse, cook, cleaner and nanny. This brings you into conflict with the Women's Libbers, but many women still agree with you.

The Ox Woman

Like your male counterpart, you are suited for a settled domestic life, preferably in the country, for you have a sensitive response to Nature. Very rarely do Ox women have a thwarted attitude towards men. Your own sexuality is strong and resilient—and while you perceive many differences between the sexes, you see them as complementary to each other rather than in direct competition.

Love and Sex

Each Ox person has a rich set of psycho-sexual emotions. You are capable of feeling much affection, much jealousy, much hatred if given sufficient cause. Once you have committed your heart, it's difficult for you to change your emotions. It isn't easy for you to talk about sex problems,

150

or to accommodate yourself to changed feelings of a partner.

BAT

10

Origins

Tenth of the 28 Chinese asterisms, situated in the Northern Palace. Chinese name: *nü* or *hsü nü*. Original meaning: a girl, or serving-maid. Position: 12° in extent, starting at ε Aquarii.

Your Emotional Nature

Bat people are hard to pin down. You do not possess many sharp, clear-cut qualities that everyone would recognise; and, indeed, you seem to change character not only in the course of a lifetime but even day by day.

So the first certain thing to be said is that you're a topsy-turvy creature, often altering your mind—for no reason as much as for good reasons—or holding diametrically opposed views at the same time. You enjoy paradox, and can turn an argument upside-down with great panache.

None of this matters very much, so long as it's kept at a trivial, humourous level. Where it can start causing trouble is in your personal relationships. Acquaintances think of you as an easy-going creature, but in close liaisons your quirky habits, noncommittal approach to decisions and difficulty in giving yourself in a wholehearted fashion all make you a slightly awkward person to live with. Not always, of course—but you need to make yourself more accommodating to other people and more prepared to pay attention to their wishes instead of simply your own.

As a youngster, you are constantly on the prowl, darting into one new experience after another in search of adventure. Your eye for detail is acute; you can spot a weak chink in a split second, and pounce on it in merciless fashion. Not that you're a cruel person by nature, nor a fanatic. But you love acting quickly in response to inner reflexes. This is why you love certain sports (field events in athletics, golf, rock climbing in particular) and why you can be so agile with your hands in do-it-yourself jobs.

As an older person, however, you seem to grow fuzzy at the edges. Your aims in life become vaguer; your once diamond-bright opinions dim into middle-of-the-road attitudes that are neither here nor there. You are quieter but still restless, like an invalid longing to go for a walk. You may well develop into a more good-natured individual than you were in your youth, but your boisterous unpredictability will have turned into middle-aged uncertainty. At this time in life, you are prone to become a religious convert, or to take up some cause not because you deeply believe in it but because you think it would help you to concentrate your energies more effectively.

The Bat Man

The male Bat enjoys the company of women so long as they are intelligent, witty and admiring . . . of him. Then he gets married, to find his greatest problem: boredom. Trap Mr Bat in a suburban semi and he nervously eyes the door. As a middle-aged man, he frequently wants to recreate his youthful escapades but usually lacks the drive to do so. He needs a shrewd, resourceful wife who will boss him in subtle ways.

The Bat Woman

Bat women, in keeping with the upside-down nature of the whole species, differ from the men in two important respects. As a mother you can take pleasure in a growing family (of boys more than girls) and have no strong desire to go on a middle-aged wander. But you enjoy committee work, or playing a vibrant part in your local social club, or engaging in voluntary charity work such as visiting the sick, or prisoners, or boarding difficult children. As a young woman, of course, your main appeal lies in your sparky personality.

Love and Sex

You make an adept lover with the right partner, but can be foiled by lack of self-confidence in new liaisons. Bat women are more sure of their femininity than Bat men of their virility, even though there's a tomboy quality about many Bat women and a certain swift grace about their menfolk.

RAT

11

Origins

Eleventh of the 28 Chinese asterisms, situated in the Northern Palace. Chinese name. *hsü*. Original meaning: emptiness. Position: 10° in extent, starting at β Aquarii.

Your Emotional Nature

You're a highly inquisitive creature with bright, clever responses. You mix easily with other people, though you tend to use people rather than make simple friendships. Always you edge towards the cynical, worldly-wise type of attitude.

You prefer the city to the countryside, a newspaper to a poem, gossip to a piece of sentiment. You flourish in business and commerce, the communications media, advertising and public relations. At worst you're an untrustworthy scoundrel who'd sell your own grandmother for a quick profit. At best, you're a delightfully witty companion who combines sharpness of mind with consideration for others.

You love taking risks, though they are always calculated ones. Often you are more concerned with the day-to-day tactics of a situation than the overall strategy. You hate being taken for a fool, yet can be surprisingly kindly to people more stupid than yourself and, if you give yourself the chance, can make a brilliant teacher.

What you need to do is bring the heart into your everyday affairs. You lack sympathy, that great liquid flow of human understanding that can alleviate sorrow and add a quality of mercy to so many situations in life.

Music is an art form that can touch your soul where mere sentimentality would not. You may be a talented singer or musician yourself, or at least have an appreciation of harmony and rhythm. In addition, you need to do a minimum of one task a day that is totally unconnected with earning money. By cultivating activities and interests which require a fairly selfless response, you can learn to counterbalance the somewhat egotistical disposition you were born with.

The Rat Male

Rats are meant to run in packs, but this isn't true of the Chinese astrological variety. You function best as a self-confident loner, rarely having trouble in your initial dealings with women but certainly not needing female company as insistently as some other types. You have a wiry charm, self-possessed and taut with energy, that appeals to many women — though others, of course, aren't fooled for a minute by your protestations of love which are so obviously part of your Grand Seduction Technique. Marriage, in the quiet suburban sense, doesn't really suit you, though you can clearly accommodate yourself to it . . . with an effort!

The Rat Female

Mrs Rat can easily become drowned in the seeming drudgery of household chores — and anticipating this, can plan to leave the marriage ship early. She needs many interests outside the home, especially a friendly but busy neighbourhood where it's easy to make new companions.

Miss Rat, as a teenager, can be very alluring, mainly because she seems to combine sex appeal with an ambitious attitude towards her career. She's on the warpath towards capturing the right husband, the richer and more promising the better.

Love and Sex

Both sexes in the Rat clan view the sex drive as just one of the weapons to use in the constant battle to stay on top in life. It's relatively easy for them to sublimate this drive in other directions—business, politics and so forth. As lovers they can be assiduous when they feel like it, but are not the world's most faithful people.

SWALLOW

12

Origins

Twelfth of the 28 Chinese asterisms, situated in the Northern Palace. Chinese name: *wei*. Original meaning: rooftop, or sharply leaning. Position: 17° in extent, starting at α Aquarii.

Your Emotional Nature

You have a sensitive disposition—sensitive towards your own feelings, towards those of other people, towards Nature and beauty and all the delicate side of life. Obviously your upbringing and everyday surroundings will have helped to shape—or hinder—this decidedly subtle, even high-strung disposition of yours . . . but it's still there, despite the fact that you may work in rather rough conditions.

Obviously you have a lot of time for other people, but that doesn't mean that you can mix all that freely with them. The fastidious side of your nature encourages you to be fussy about whom you like, whom you can't stand, and whom you can just about tolerate.

In other words, you want to be friendly, but the finely honed quality of your emotional demeanour means that some people—well, quite a number, to be truthful—simply aren't your type. It's very important, with your kind of emotional nature, that you keep this fastidiousness within sensible bounds. If you surrender to it, you'll find yourself like a little old spinster lady, ever so affable in the street but never ever inviting anyone home.

At your best, you have genuine charm. People will pull themselves together, so to speak, and project a more rarefied, cultured side of them in your presence. But you make a fatal mistake if you try to lead a life full of Beauty, Taste and Charm, all with capital letters. Then you appear genteel, like Lily Tomalin in *Laugh-In*, smirking with pleasure at your own ever-so-nice manners and, by implication, sneering at other people's.

The other potential fault with your kind of disposition is that you don't stand up for yourself. Your typical emotional response is to try, straight away, to reach a halfway compromise; so that in the hands of a really tough operator, you constantly give way, yield, back down and make further compromises until, frankly, you've nothing left to bargain with.

The Swallow Male

Obviously the man of the species is a bit of a ladies' man. At worst he simpers and gushes in a terribly camp way, but more normally he simply has a way with women; in him they sense a kindred spirit who understands their problems and wants to sympathise with them. Other men, meanwhile, and indeed some butch women, are liable to tease him for his graceful manners; but the times they are a-changing, and we now recognise that we all possess a balance of male-female hormones and aren't exclusively one or the other.

The Lady Swallow

You exude a refined, beauty-loving, artistic set of sensibilities, so are more suited to drawing-room-style courtship than a heavy spell of nappy-washing before feeding the rest of the family. You mustn't allow your 'precious' quality to turn you puritan—equally, you mustn't, as an unmarried girl, be so picky-and-choosy that you never pick a husband at all.

Love and Sex

Yours is not a particularly sensual love-nature in the rude, robust, Chaucerian meaning. In certain ways you edge towards a romantic, spiritual kind of love that never gets too physical. Your sex drive tends to get redirected into other fields: design, art appreciation, a love of flowers. Thus you need a partner who both understands this delicacy of approach yet can coax you out of it. You remain loyal to a loving partner, can seem to tolerate an unloving one for a long time, but are a bit fearful of swapping partners.

BOAR 13

Origins

Thirteenth of the 28 Chinese asterisms, situated in the Northern Palace. Chinese name: *shih* or *ying shih*. Original meaning: the mansion, or encampment. Position: 16° in extent, starting at α Pegasi.

Your Emotional Nature

You're a mass of contradictory reactions to life. In some ways, especially when your intellectual interest is aroused, you develop great driving-force. Yet in others, when you are bored or self-obsessed, you turn downright lazy and even slovenly in your habits and emotional attitudes.

A similar contrast can be seen in your approach to other people. If they have something you want, or if there's just one item in their psychological armoury that attracts you, then you display considerable interest; and similarly, in a selfish way, if there's one aspect of their lives that rouses your crusading spirit—be it of anger or enthusiasm—then you pay a great deal of attention to them and their problems. But with people you know well, be they relatives or neighbours or the actual marriage partner, you allow the familiarity to turn into a mild contempt . . . or at least, into behaviour that borders on indifference. With close relationships, once the initial excitement has worn off, you tend to take them for granted . . . and every so often—like now!—you need waking up and told: 'Boar, you're a bit of a bore!'

It's a hit-n-miss question whether you strike up a friendship with a new acquaintance. Sometimes you can be full of enthusiasm, at other times quite unmoved by their presence. If you didn't have such a sharp brain, people would call you a moody person. As it is, you really do get to grips with certain ideas, concentrating fiercely on them; then you lapse back into a more relaxed, easy-going, slouchy sort of emotional posture.

The same eager–lazy syndrome can be seen in your approach to marriage. You seem to combine sensuality with a can't-be-bothered attitude. A love affair that took you out of yourself would be a real puzzling experience to you, who normally like to be highly inquisitive about other people but quite unselfconscious about your own feelings.

The Male Boar

It's easy to allow the sensuous side of your nature to develop into a kind of promiscuous tic, even if only in the imagination. But to give you an alluring *femme fatale* for a wife would be quite wrong. You need a sensible, attractive, middle-of-the-road kind of wife who will tolerate your ups and downs and still be a good companion. She is the woman who can bring out the best in you: endurance, mental stimulation, a willingness to help people who find themselves in trouble through no fault of their own.

The Boar Woman

Unless you're the real blue-stocking type of girl who's an intellectual cut above the rest of us, you bring a good deal more charm and perky attractiveness to your everyday disposition than does your male counterpart. It's only as middle age sets in—and it can start early, you know!—that the slightly sarky, deprecating side of your nature comes through . . . and by then, hopefully, you have established enough of a well-rounded emotional life to dispel the sour taste of this side of your personality. Your best points are a willingness to work hard in the dutiful role as mother and housewife even though you really need more than mere dusting and polishing to maintain your mind at its full potential, and a capacity, every so often, to take the lead in community affairs and create a stink about some local government abuse.

Love and Sex

As already indicated, Boars are lusty creatures, so a cold partner will never suit you. If anything, you need someone who can bring you out of any sloth in which you might have sunk and maintain your interest in yourself and the relationship. This is particularly important after a few years of marriage when the glamour's worn off. Then you either sink into a slow decline or start looking for fun elsewhere—when all along the real answer lies in having the courage to resuscitate the marriage itself.

PORCUPINE 14

Origins

Fourteenth of the 28 Chinese asterisms, situated in the Northern Palace. Chinese name: *pi* or *tung pi*. Original meaning: a wall, or Eastern wall. Position: 9° in extent, starting at γ Pegasi.

Your Emotional Nature

Sometimes, like a real porcupine in Nature, you seem more prickly than you really are. The truth is that you have a very soft nature. Some Porcupines, mainly the menfolk, feel a need to disguise their genuine sensitivity with an outer display of tetchy, tough temper, but it really is a nonsense, and they don't mean it.

Porcupines, at their best, have a deep love of home, family and a few close friends. This will come through in an interest in genealogy, family trees, old gravestones and other relics of the past. You'll love heirlooms, family photographs, Granny's old sofa and, of course, will have the fondest memories of the house and garden where you were brought up, plus the neighbours, your own childhood pals and the smells and sights of all your early life.

Your soft heart is ever-ready with sympathy and concern and interest for other people. Except for shyness, which can inhibit you on occasion, there's nothing to prevent you making many friends. But in the last resort you seem to prefer a small clan of really close buddies. With them you can be totally honest, revealing, rather like someone in the confessional, all your inner feelings and desires and worries. You love nothing better than having a proper heart-to-heart chat, for you have a rich imagination and something of a dramatic temperament that needs to paint your inner feelings with some theatrical colour, even exaggeration. It's not that you lie—well, only occasionally! — but like to dress up reality in the clothes of vivid fantasy.

The Porcupine Male

It's sometimes a bit hard for the male Porcupine to find the right men friends with whom to have this close, heart-felt relationship. So he falls back on women, a tendency much helped by the close relationship he's liable to develop with his mother in his early years. She greatly affects his emotional likes and dislikes and everyday reactions. The women he's sexually attracted to will have some kind of link with his image of his mother; and her views and attitudes and opinions will all be mirrored, in some way, in his own views. Obviously, especially around adolescence, the Porcupine boy tries to fight clear of this maternal influence . . . but he'll never be entirely free of it.

The Porcupine Woman

The Porcupine emotional nature suits a woman's life-style well. She's a maternal type herself, loving children around her; and other people warm to the gentle, understanding quality of her psyche.

As a young girl, the Porcupine has difficulty knowing her own feelings. She can easily be swept off her feet by a crafty seducer, and a sad, disillusioning experience early in her love life can make her more wary than by nature she is.

Love and Sex

Porcupines respond well to sexual feelings, but are pretty hopeless at casual encounters. You're ideal marriage fodder, and should think early of looking for the right husband and wife and indicating that they want it to last for keeps.

WOLF 15

Origins

Fifteenth of the 28 Chinese asterisms, situated in the Western Palace. Chinese name: *khuei*. Original meaning: legs. Position: 16° in extent, starting at η Andromedae.

Your Emotional Nature

You seem to have courage, a crusading spirit, psychic energy and a good attack on life that wakes you up early in the morning and keeps you going all day. Your normal response to life is bright, snappy, a bit guileful and tricky at times, but essentially straightforward.

Some people might think there's a touch of the manic-depressive about you, for you can veer from enthusiasm to gloom in a matter of minutes. The gloom, however, is never real gloomy gloom; it's theatrical gloom, all heavy dark blue thunder clouds that are pretty rather than threatening. Hence, maybe, an echo of the small boy who shouted 'Wolf! wolf!' so often that nobody believed him. In the same way, you seem to enjoy your disasters so much that people learn not to take them seriously. (One day, of course, the wolf actually arrived in the village—so maybe, when you really get sincerely low, it's made worse by friends thinking you're just having a bit of a moodie.)

If you are in doubt, you fall back on what Daddy (or some other figure of authority) told you to think. For in the final analysis, you are not as invincible and self-sufficient as you like to believe. It means that you really need some kind of moral belief to back up your judgments— a faith that reinforces your arguments with an absolute inner certainty that such-and-such really is so.

Your strength of mind is a bit of a sham (but none the worse for that). In reality, you need a partner with whom to share your life.

The Wolf Male

In your bachelor days you may adopt the wolf-whistle approach to girls, but it isn't really true of your emotional nature. Certainly you're attracted by the female personality and looks, but you're the sort of man who basically wants to settle down, not into dullness but into maturity. Casual sex relationships bore you, because they are so superficial; the longer kind of affair, lasting a year or two, is better; but best of all is a marriage that stays physically alive but is reinforced with plenty of rich, understanding emotional familiarity.

The Wolf Woman

As a young woman you enjoy being an attractive creature who can turn men's heads, not to mention their hearts. Although you settle into marriage happily enough (with the right man, of course!) you're not the world's most motherly mother. You don't want children hanging round your skirts all the time; you prefer children as youngsters, out and about in the countryside, having fun as a family but leaving you time to enjoy other interests besides cooking, cleaning and coping with cuts and bruises.

Love and Sex

Clearly the Wolf nature responds to sexual feelings, but always wants to go beyond them into a deeper commitment. You should avoid really dull, stolid partners; you need someone who combines a sense of fun with an air of responsibility, who treats life as an enjoyable activity which is not trivial, not solemn, but halfway between.

DOG

Origins

Sixteenth of the 28 Chinese asterisms, situated in the Western Palace. Chinese name: *lou*. Original meaning: the tether. Position: 12° in extent, starting at β Arietis.

Your Emotional Nature

Your usual response to life is an intelligent, practical, no-nonsense one. You're intrigued by problems and enjoy solving them, but nobody would call you an outstandingly inventive or original person. Your satisfactions are quiet ones, your desires not notably strong or unusual. You are, in short, the average man or woman.

This needn't make you dull; simply an all-rounder of moderate views who is prepared to accommodate others provided they will make some move in your direction, too.

You rarely grab the headlines or try to dominate a conversation—though, if severely provoked, a dogged determination to put the plain-man's point of view will become evident. Not a fanatic by any means, your emotional peace of mind rests on certain well-established truths, and if these are questioned or challenged for long enough, your normal tolerance gives way to an outraged, baffled cry that the world's going crazy.

Your trouble is distinguishing truth from bias. The older you get, the more you are liable to believe that what you've become used to must, almost by natural law, be 'right'. You run the danger, in fact, of becoming an old square—hence the appositeness of the old saw 'You can't teach an old Dog new tricks.'

People find they can trust you, so you develop a fatherly image in the course of a lifetime. But they can also disregard you, which is a pity for you have learnt through experience to become an understanding, well rounded individual.

The Dog Male

The young male Dog has plenty of puppy-like energy directed towards the female of the species. This is a fairly uncritical, straightforward kind of sexual drive, and the trouble with it is that it can be a little insensitive. But there's little real aggression in a puppy, and certainly no cruelty; as you grow older, you develop into a responsible family man certainly capable of enjoying a boisterous physical relationship but not wanting to look further than his spouse for satisfaction.

Obviously you want a similarly undemonstrative person as wife, though then you run the danger of becoming a boring couple. The flirty, restless type isn't for you.

The Lady Dog

No, you're not the bitchy sort! Your splendid good humour and understanding manner help you to steer clear of the sour rocks that can wreck relationships. In anything, your danger is taking your husband too much for granted, and, perhaps, yourself as well. You need regular boosts to your ego to get you out of the rut that may be pleasant and cosy . . . but is still a rut.

Love and Sex

Dylan Thomas wrote a short story *Just Like Little Dogs* which might be true of Swansea teenage love lives but not, repeat not, of the Dog nature in Chinese astrology. You look for a calm, permanent love relationship with a person you can respect as well as feel fond of. The only kind of Dog person capable of enjoying many lovers is the self-contained adult bachelor . . . but even there, he's missing out.

You're more likely to feel hurt than jealous if your partner ran away with someone else.

PHEASANT   17

Origins

Seventeenth of the 28 Chinese asterisms, situated in the Western Palace. Chinese name: *wei*. Original meaning: the stomach. Position: 14° in extent, starting at 41 Arietis.

Your Emotional Nature

Thus *hsui* originally meant the stomach, which gives a surprisingly apt summary of your emotional response to life. Far from being an impulsive, volatile, lively and superficial sort of individual, you like to digest experience before coming to any judgment about it. You pause, you mentally masticate, you weigh and consider before delivering yourself of your emotional response to the situation.

At worst, this means that all your feelings and sentiments are terribly bland, a sort of emotional stodge. The older some Pheasants get, the more chewed-over and familiar their opinions become; they have an awful habit of repeating the same anecdotes to the same company.

At best, however, you bring an accumulated experience to all your remarks. As a food, pheasant is ripe and spicy, and there's a similar maturity and richness to your reactions to life.

The stomach is also the psychic nerve-centre of the whole organism, which is why people talk about butterflies in the tummy when they're scared. You do not frighten easily, but in your slow, steady way you are much more percipient than an outsider would give you credit for. It manifests partly in your ability to appreciate music and, indeed, your skill in singing or playing a musical instrument.

You don't make friends quickly (you don't really react quickly to much!) but you're unfriendly to virtually no-one, and, if you're true to the Pheasant ideal, hardly anyone will be unfriendly towards you. Your faults, as far as your general emotional disposition is concerned, are a tendency to be tiresomely avuncular and pompous, and, perhaps, a tendency to avoid hostility too much. Nobody likes to get in the way of an angry person—and while you don't exactly run away, you do step adroitly aside . . . and some might see this as a form of cowardice.

The Pheasant Male

You're proud of your virility, and have no objection to displaying it, so to speak, in the form of gorgeous clothes, prestige cars and all the other accoutrements of the 20th-century trendy male.

You aren't the type who can contentedly slip back into suburban domesticity and say goodbye to any further flirtation once you are married. You need to lead an active social life with an opportunity to mix with pretty women, and you want your own wife to flourish in her own right rather than simply as mother to your children.

The Lady Pheasant

You have a vivacious response to life—and men!—and are certainly a sensuous woman. If spurned or misused, your high spirits turn into revenge. But in a contented love relationship, you have a fine capacity to revel in the familiarity of the partner so long as the pair of you maintain a style and élan between you.

Love and Sex

Pheasants enjoy all the bodily comforts, not least among them the joy of physical love. The young Pheasant needs the opportunity to have his or her moment of glory before settling down into matrimony. And there's no doubt that in early middle age the Pheasant can develop a roving eye.

COCK   18

Origins

Eighteenth of the 28 Chinese asterisms, situated in the Western Palace. Chinese name: *mao*. Original meaning: a star-map showing the Pleiades. Position: 11° in extent, starting at η Tauri.

Your Emotional Nature

Your immediate response to life—and 'immediate' may be understating the speed of your reactions—is that you want to take charge of the situation. If your opinion is asked, you give it tersely and vividly; if a judgment is required, you supply it, whether or not you really have enough evidence to make a fair decision. Above all, if something has to be *done*, instead of merely talking about it, you relish the prospect, for your whole emotional disposition is geared to the task of tackling problems in as speedy and straightforward a manner as possible.

You give orders to yourself, but better still, you like giving orders to others. And by and large, it's fair to add that at your best, you're quite a pleasant person to take orders from. There is an air of natural authority and leadership about your personality that seems to make the rest of us jump to it.

At your worst, of course, you're quite insufferable, puffing out your chest with ridiculous pride, unable to laugh at yourself and accept a subordinate role in the scheme of things.

You do enjoy being king of the castle. It's this itch for power and importance that sets you going. Left to your own devices for any length of time, you can become lazy, sorry for yourself and frustrated. On a desert island, alone and needing to be self-sufficient, you might easily go to pieces.

Obviously you mix well with people, so long as they'll accept you on your terms. You cannot make important compromises willingly, and sometimes it's for your own good that you get a little comeuppance.

The Cock Male

The male hormones really have the scene pretty much to themselves, and it's up to you to train yourself to be a bit more feminine than your actual emotional disposition allows. Otherwise you constantly have to go around conquering people (especially ladies) all the time, proving your manhood whenever an opportunity arises. Even late in life, you're still showing off your bronzed body at swimming pools. You ought to study flower arrangement or some other artistic pursuit.

The Lady Cock

It's still a vivid, full-of-personality kind of emotional life that you lead, but you project a kind of rigorous femininity. You demand attention, and if men don't seem to be paying enough attention, you have plenty of tricks to make them keep their eyes on you. You may not be a woman's woman in the sense of loving cosy neighbourly chats over the garden fence, but many women admire you, secretly or otherwise, and can establish very good relationships with you.

Love and Sex

. It must be quite clear that the Cock person has a vivid sexuality demanding adequate release. Interestingly enough, however, you are so full of energy that the sex drive can be diverted, for a while at least, into other channels: sport, a career of responsibility, anger against other people, even.

Your trouble is always that you are more intent on projecting your own loveliness than admiring your partner's. It's easy for you to kid yourself that you are tremendously attentive to the other person when, quite frankly, you are simply satisfying your own urges. Love—real sweet humble human love—is not an easy emotion for you to grasp . . . but if it does come your way, you have the single-mindedness of purpose to pursue it and make it your own.

RAVEN 19

Origins

Nineteenth of the 28 Chinese asterisms, situated in the Western Palace. Chinese name: *pi*. Original meaning: a net, or writing tablet. Position: 16° in extent, starting at ε Tauri.

Your Emotional Nature

You are the natural clerk or secretary: tidy, meticulous in your habits, worrying when details are perfect, undemanding and uncomplaining and prepared to take a back-seat while someone else receives all the glory.

This doesn't mean that you don't have a decent ration of personal pride—indeed, you can be very pleased with yourself in certain ways, only you demurely try to keep these boastful feelings to yourself. That's both your asset and disadvantage. Nearly all of us recognise the virtue of modesty, which you possess in full measure; most of us feel that false modesty, of which you are capable, is a silly, hypocritical emotion; and some of us detect, in your grin-and-bear-it attitude, an element of cowardice, a fear of being truly yourself, a backing-away from the harsh realities of life. Just as the secretary in an office cannot function without a figure of authority to sanction her actions, so you, in some of your emotional reactions to life, sometimes seem as though you are saying 'No' because you haven't the self-confidence to say 'Yes'.

At your best, you can be an angel of sweetness and utility. If people want help, there you are to supply assistance. If there's a long, laborious and routine task to be tackled, call in Raven! Not that you're a monotony seeker, far from it. You love a lot of variety in life, but your built-in predisposition to obey an order, do your duty and provide a service to others encourages you to accept a sacrifice, if need be, and to make a good job of it, too.

You mix quite well, in your shy way, with all sorts of people—though you take your time in appraising them, to see whether they suit you or not.

The Raven Male

Girls are attracted to you for a variety of reasons: your bright brain, your ambition, your beady charm, your male crispness of manner. But rarely, to be honest, for your overt sex appeal, for it simply isn't there. You aren't the sort of bloke parading it round the streets; it exists, have no doubt about that (as if you did!). It's just hiding under a bushel.

You are strong in loyalty, responsibility, principles, honour and fond regard. You don't often, past your adolescence, get carried away by love. You need a girl who needs a man like you—and if that sounds calculating . . . well, you are an astute, calculating sort of man.

The Lady Raven

You can be quite striking in appearance and appeal, but like your male counterpart, you don't really have the IT of film-star glamour. You adopt a fairly businesslike approach to life, and certainly seek an ambitious husband with the ability to get ahead. At worst, you turn into a nagger and shrew and grouchy old pecksniff. At best, you're the salt of the earth: plain, wholesome, yet giving a crisp savour to every activity with which you come into contact.

Love and Sex

Ravens have a slightly snooty, distant air about them, but when the mood strikes them they can be pretty sexy! You may have some tendency to get obsessed with the techniques of sex, and, indeed, to treat the exercise as just that—nice healthy exercise.

MONKEY 20

Origins

Twentieth of the 28 Chinese asterisms, situated in the Western Palace. Chinese name: *tsui* or *tsui chui*. Original meaning: lips or turtle. Position: 2° in extent, starting at λ Orionis.

Your Emotional Nature

Wow! Life is so fabulous and stimulating for you that you can hardly pause for breath. Quick, over there! Something new! Drop what you're doing, hop across to see. Now something else! Hurry, hurry! There's no time to finish that—move on to the new job/person/idea/joke/TV channel/friendship.

You may not be quite so frenetic as that, but as caricatures go—and you love caricatures!—it captures the essence of your response to life.

You're like a telephone exchange, only awake if you've plenty of incoming and outgoing calls. You're a jangle of nerve-endings, immensely alive to the least tremor around you. You adore changes, need fresh stimulation, welcome the opportunity to turn the next corner or advance over the brow of the hill. Surprises were invented to suit your palate; you loathe monotony, and cannot understand people who are content to do the same old thing, week after week.

Monkeys move in packs. You hate being alone, you must constantly relate to your environment (even in an empty room you have to touch the furniture, to reassure yourself that you still 'belong'). This is why there's a compulsion for you to make friends and strike up acquaintances, the more the merrier. You like to keep life at a superficial level. Serious relationships worry you; they make demands, they impose duties, and you prefer to stay free and unbeholden.

Your faults are obvious: a basic cowardice, the ability to change your mind to suit each fleeting twist of fortune, your lack of stamina. But your virtues are shining: a lovely ability to make people laugh, cry and applaud; a good inquisitive mind that's inventive and resourceful; and a young-at-heart emotional disposition that always makes your manner seem less than your years.

The Male Monkey

Your perennial difficulty is growing up. You hate to do it, with the consequence that you seem boyish and precocious, even in middle-age. You enjoy playing the role of the bright, up-and-coming youngster, and you need an older male figure or two in your life who can play kindly, amused father to your impertinent adolescent.

It's the same with women. You have the best compatibility with girls like yourself—clever, frisky, putting on a show— yet seem ineluctably drawn towards the strong woman who can take care of life's little obligations while you enjoy yourself.

The Monkey Woman

You retain your freshness of reaction throughout life, but it suits a feminine temperament. The responsibilities of marriage and motherhood can dishearten you at first; but you are wonderfully adaptable, and so long as you can introduce plenty of spice and variety into your domestic life, you stay happy enough—happier than working at a boring factory assembly line.

You feel safe with a capable, responsible man—if not a father figure then an elder-brother figure. But that type sometimes proves restrictive, and the whole moral challenge of your life is the need to take a bit of weight on your own shoulders and learn how to adopt a caring attitude.

Love and Sex

The Monkey approach to these matters is lightweight, flirtatious, unserious—like a romp on the ottoman. You are more inclined to infatuation than real passion, to intrigue than open commitment, to variety instead of monogamy. Obviously you can learn to be faithful, but it's not the most natural attitude in the world for you to hold.

APE 21

Origins

Twenty-first of the 28 Chinese asterisms, situated in the Western Palace. Chinese name: *shen*. Original meaning: a star-map of three stars. Position: 9° in extent, starting at ζ Orionis.

Your Emotional Nature

You're a good deal more serious than the flotsam and jetsam of the Monkeys (No 20 above), but you still share certain common responses to life. You have a lively, restless emotional disposition that is keenly inquisitive, about other people, about the secrets of Nature (including human nature) and about public affairs. You mix well, but are capable of forming more serious relationships than can a Monkey.

This makes you a clever person who needs to use your brain at work if you're to be properly fulfilled. You need to use it in your leisure-hours, too, in some absorbing hobby—anything from stamp-collecting to amateur geology.

If people ask you a question, they can almost hear your mental processes at work. You're a great ponderer, skipping from one answer to the next but never replying impulsively, like the Monkey would do. Apes make great chess players; you're good at looking ahead, planning the next ten moves but not ruining the game by getting childishly excited. You make good politicians, too, with your combination of executive judgment and fluency with words.

You love the truth, and hate lies, but sometimes see the necessity for telling falsehoods. You act like a person intrigued by the possibility of organising your life in the light of a moral code, in search of the right one to suit you, but still keeping an open mind. It's an attractive attitude, and people will like you for your personal qualities as well as your intellectual gifts. Perhaps the nub of it is: you seem trustworthy and likeable—a rare combination!

The Ape Man

The Ape characteristics suit the male temperament well. They help you to flourish in professions like the Bar, sales, and administration where the gift of the gab needs to be balanced by common-sense and technical know-how.

You're a sexual animal, versatile but capable of a lasting love. It's hard—indeed, impossible—to summarise the kind of woman that suits you best, because you really need three or four different feminine types to satisfy the various facets of your psycho-sexual temperament. You may not want to make love to them all; in fact, you're the kind of man who is capable of platonic male–female relationships. You enjoy a clubby atmosphere where the sexes can get together in a friendly atmosphere.

The Ape Woman

You have a lot of charm—part of it your natural endowment, part of it gained through experience in the world: experience in handling people, almost in exercising professional charm.

You like *interesting* men: perhaps your actual egghead, at least men who have travelled and can recount a good story, with whom you can enjoy an intellectual relationship as well as a physical one. You see the tasks of motherhood as essentially educating your children to be self-sufficient, lively and intelligent adults. There is very little possessiveness in your nature, and you hardly know what it's like to be jealous. Offended at a betrayal of trust, yes—but not the mad baying of the atavistic gut.

Love and Sex

Friendly, capable of a range of well-rounded relationships, you feel at home in the late 20th-century world of fluctuating liaisons and absence of class antagonisms.

TAPIR 22

Origins

Twenty-second of the 28 Chinese asterisms, situated in the Southern Palace. Chinese name: *ching* or *tung ching*. Original meaning: the well. Position: 33° in extent, starting at μ Geminorum.

Your Emotional Nature

At your best, there's a kind of wise stillness within your nature that's extremely comforting to most other people. Not all—some people will find you annoyingly slow in some of your reactions; but that's their loss.

You work better as a personality in your middle and later years than in your youth. You need time in which to sieve the good from the worthless, the true from the misleading. As a teenager you may seem a bit callow; but with age you seem able to refine experience down to the essentials. What's more, you have the means of expressing yourself, often in calm yet precise cadences, so that you can criticise with sympathy, and nurture people intelligently.

In short, you combine wisdom with motherliness.

In the course of a lifetime you develop a marvellous memory. You're likely to be attracted to history, and therefore are able to place our own times in a long-term perspective. This is irritating to the trendy young who think they've just discovered it all for the first time—but people looking for real balanced advice will know your virtues.

It's true that your kind of attitude can lead to smugness. You must be prepared to rethink your views in the light of a new generation, but mustn't go so far as to lose the value of your own predisposition.

You expect people to meet you largely on your own terms. You set the standards—and can be mightily efficient, in your quiet way, in maintaining them—and while staying marvellously tolerant of the rest of humankind, do tend, especially as you get older, to keep yourself to yourself.

The Male Tapir

The extrovert Tapir flourishes in well-ordered societies, especially in those devoted to learning like schools and universities. He has ambitions, but not the orthodox ones of monetary success and respectability. He responds to inner standards—and it's the same with his approach to women. He is never so crude that he wants nothing but conquest. He prefers a subtle, teasing approach. He never feels entirely at home in a purely emotional environment. He needs a witty, self-aware approach to love.

The introvert Tapir is definitely shy. He will prefer a strong-minded woman who can run the mundane details of his own life as well as leading a fairly independent life herself.

The Tapir Woman

You're the sensible, motherly type. You aren't flashy or flirtatious, though you enjoy a good joke and can generate a lot of fun within a small familiar group such as the family circle. You need a man you can both admire and help: no-one too dominant or self-sufficient, but not helpless either.

Love and Sex

The typical Tapir is a person of sensibilities rather than sensuality: civilised not crude, able to sublimate desires if need be but certainly capable of a full, lasting love. You seek a loving companion, for you do not like to lose control of your own intelligence. There may be a certain lack of drive in courtship and marriage that can take too much for granted; but once reminded of your lapses, your sensitive heart quickly responds to the needs of your partner.

SHEEP   23

Origins

Twenty-third of the 28 Chinese asterisms, situated in the Southern Palace. Chinese name: *kuei* or *yü kuei*. Original meaning: spirits, ghosts or ghost-vehicle. Position: 4° in extent, starting at *θ* Cancri.

Your Emotional Nature

There are two important aspects to your emotional disposition. One side of you wants to react to life in a clear, capable, practical and commonsensical way. You admire people of experience and judgment, and seek to be the same kind of person in your heart.

The other side of you—which may not be so strongly

emphasised, but exists nonetheless—is much more sensitive, even psychic. It's like fly-paper, picking up passing impressions, absorbing the atmosphere of places and people, registering unspoken thoughts unconsciously yet mysteriously taking them into account when making decisions.

This combination of tough and soft, materialistic and spiritual, down-to-earth and up-in-the-air, makes you a surprisingly difficult person to get to know, even by close friends. Nobody—perhaps including yourself—can be sure which way you'll respond to a given situation. Sometimes the sensible Sheep nature will take command, making you seem an ordinary, businesslike individual. Then, out of the blue, you'll react much more percipiently: positively, by seeing through a complex problem right to its essential core—or, more negatively, by turning touchy, abruptly taking offence where none was intended.

Equally, it's hard to know with Sheep whether they'll be amiable or solitary. Some Sheep are decidedly gregarious, with the self-confidence to hold their own in company; they enjoy other people, especially self-made men, pretty women and children of all ages, in a hearty way. But other Sheep, whose sensitive side is stressed, shy away from people. They realise how easily—and maybe disastrously—they can be moved by mass emotions, whether they stem from a grand State occasion, a Salvation Army band, or a football crowd.

You do not have particularly brave instincts. Certainly there's no great impulse to be original, or to go out on a limb in defence of an unorthodox idea. You rather distrust 'clever' people, and as you grow older you tend to grow more conservative in your emotional attitudes.

The Male Sheep

You look for loyalty and faithfulness in a wife—a woman who can rear your children with decency, efficiency and love. You are not a flirty, lighthearted man yourself, though you may enjoy a bit of fun. Essentially you're a solid man of the world, who must think of your social position before doing anything 'silly'.

Women like you for your air of dependability—and, of course, your practical skills that enable you to earn the money to provide the domestic comforts in life. The danger you are tempted to make is to contract a marriage of convenience—or, worse still, a 'good' marriage that is based more on class, money and property than love for the girl herself.

The Woman Sheep

At your best, you combine warmth of manner with plenty of good sense. Obviously you want a husband with good prospects; obviously, too, you want security of affection within marriage. But if you marry too stolid and upright a man, there's a danger that your combined weight (psychologically speaking!) will drag the union down into dullness and mutual indifference. It's probably better for you to look for the attractive outsider, in the marriage stakes, than automatically plump for the top-weight favourite. It presents you with a greater challenge.

Love and Sex

Bright and eager in youth; familiar but a mite boring in your middle years; absent in old age—that's how the Sheep psycho-sexual pattern looks. It's up to you to keep it bright and eager throughout life—by staying young in heart!

MUNTJAK 24

Origins

Twenty-fourth of the 28 Chinese asterisms, situated in the Southern Palace. Chinese name: *liu*. Original meaning: the willow tree. Position: 15° in extent, starting at δ Hydrae.

Your Emotional Nature

You have a 'pretty' disposition: graceful, companionable and a little helpless. Your natural instinct is to make yourself appear as attractive to others as possible—not a bad attitude, by any means, but one that relies on *their* estimation of you. You may begin by seeming to set your own standards; but pretty soon you are slavishly following other people's fashions.

This image of you as victim of society's demands is a somewhat negative picture of you at your best: a friendly, eager-to-please individual who is keenly aware of how other people feel. You seem to come truly alive only when other people are present. On a desert island, you would not only be impractical to the point of inertia; you might die of loneliness.

It's fair to call you a drawing-room sort of person. You like 'nice' neighbours and friends, and tend to ignore, sometimes quite deliberately, the uglier side of life. Your motives, here, you tell yourself, are transparently pure; by thinking positively, you help to create the positive surroundings in real life. But this is your basic trouble. You are adept at finding what you consider to be good excuses for leading a way of life that is pleasant and agreeable and, above all, irresponsible. By following the dictates of society, you are absolved from personal obligation.

Ultimate ethics apart, you are a very charming individual in your manners and general deportment. You are marvellous at finding the right words to bring two warring partners together.

The Male Muntjak

Your basic narcissisism can be tempered with genuine regard for other people's feelings, but you always run the risk of being thought too fond of yourself. As far as women are concerned, you like to see them partly as adorable, pretty creatures: a decoration that reflects on your own taste. And partly as delightful companions with whom you can share intimate conversations.

This dolly-bird image of women is immature. What you really need is a relatively efficient wife who can organise herself—and you!—and who doesn't need a strong, dominant male presence ordering her about.

The Lady Muntjak

The same applies to you. You run the risk of being vain and selfish, and there's no doubt that you get on well with the softer type of man: the ladies' man, in short. But you really need a capable husband who provides you with the support and encouragement . . . encouragement, in fact, to stand more on your own two pretty feet than you really want to.

Love and Sex

The Muntjak operates a great deal through the senses. So you're a refined sexual animal, glad to express love through bodily affection; yet still capable of transcending pure desire and appreciating spiritual love.

Courtesy cannot, by your standards, be separated from affection. To love someone is to feel polite respect for him or her. Of course you treasure the deeper feelings, too: loyalty, the passion of togetherness, the ties that come with familiarity. But in the last resort you cannot associate with anyone who is not, in some measure, cultivated. This can lead to a kind of sexual snobbery—but at its sweetest, it's an attitude that makes the world a more desirable place in which to live.

HORSE 25

Origins

Twenty-fifth of the 28 Chinese asterisms, situated in the Southern Palace. Chinese name: *hsing* or *chhi hsing*.

Original meaning: the star, or the Seven Stars. Position: 7° in extent, starting at α Hydrae.

Your Emotional Nature

You have the inner nature of the managing director. Your instincts, your typical responses to life, your moods and the way you master them—all these are indicative of a person who wants to get a grip on their life . . . and, frankly, likes to feel the reins of power in their hands.

You have no special need to throw your weight around, or boast, or do any of the extrovert things that insecure people do to make them feel they belong. Since birth you've always felt you belonged . . . up there, at the top, where the decisions are made. And your inner emotional disposition has always edged you to assume a position of power and responsibility, in however small a way.

The head executive of a company has vision, skill, ability to pay attention to details, and, above all, the courage to make decisions. In the same way, when you are confronted by a problem, your instincts tell you to know all the facts, to put them in a sensible order, to see them as part of an overall policy of objectives in your life, and then to make up your mind as speedily as possible. As a Horse person, you combine efficiency with cheerfulness. You love the sensation of taking risks that you know are based on facts.

In your social life, you mix easily with a wide range of people—but always, you seek to impose, in however subtle a way, your views or personality on the relationship. It may not be at all obvious, but it's certainly the way you inwardly wish to operate.

Vision you have; imagination, which is a more emotional quality, you may lack. You can sometimes treat other people as machines who should work at your bidding. And sometimes you miss the whole point of a play, or conversation, or intimate relationship, because you lack the right antennae.

The Male Horse

You know your own mind, have your own tastes, want to get your own way—but you want to do it in a relatively unobtrusive manner. Women, to you, are part playthings, part necessary accoutrement to the well-set-up man. You want to make a good marriage, just as you want everything you touch to be quality. The actual feelings of the woman you marry, the normal give-and-take of matrimony —these could be a closed book to you. You're certainly capable of engineering the love and admiration of many women; but whether you'll allow yourself to be genuinely moved by one is another matter.

The Lady Horse

There's a cheerful, exuberant side to your nature in youth. Once married, you tackle the tasks of mother and housewife with swift efficiency, leaving you time for the more important matters of fashion, social engagements and playing a role in the local community. You can build up such a 'public', well-groomed image that people may wonder—correctly—whether you have any quiet, simple, private life left.

Love and Sex

The Horse, of both sexes, is a sensual animal, but the sexual feelings need not be allied to genuine human affection. Although faithful by nature, you have the disposition to seek pleasure elsewhere than an unhappy marriage bed.

DEER   26

Origins

Twenty-sixth of the 28 Chinese asterisms, situated in the Southern Palace. Chinese name: *chang*. Original meaning: an extended net, or hornless deer. Position: 18° in extent, starting at μ Hydrae.

Your Emotional Nature

Broadcaster, publisher, towncrier, local gossip: these are the ideal vocations for you. You love telling people the good news, any news, so long as people are interested and you are relaying the information. It needn't be the absolute truth either—though you draw the line at utter lies.

That, at any rate, is your average, coarse, workaday Deer. A more refined version, frequently to be seen at poetry recitals, has a languid charm. There's still the same delight in words, though no longer quite for their own sake. An element of soul has entered, a genuine feeling for the inner beauty of life.

You are clearly drawn to the cultivated side of life, and even if you have little money, you still manage to turn out attractively, both in appearance and personality. You are not really an egotist, in a greedy, aren't-I-marvellous? sense. But you have no intention of taking a back seat.

You operate in the world of inner values. You do not care to measure in a precise way; you weigh and compare according to your subjective feelings. Does such-and-such improve the quality of life? is a more apposite question to you than 'Will it be profitable?'. You are not really interested in practical, materialist considerations very much: far more in the looks and styling of experience.

Most Deer mix incredibly well, unless it's very alien company where you feel unsure of yourself. Nobody could call you physically brave, but you have the courage of your own opinions: a kind of steely independence of thought that won't accept the common received wisdom.

The Male Deer

You come in two varieties. The first, relatively extrovert type is self-assured in company, nobody's fool, appreciative of women's qualities but capable of remaining free of emotional entanglements unless it definitely suits your book to become involved. Many actors are this kind of Deer by emotional preference.

The shyer version, perhaps due to an over-stressed relationship with the mother, is much more dependent on the love of a woman, yet, by nature, more frightened of it. This kind of Deer isn't forceful enough, is sensitive to the point of physical sickness, and should learn to have enough confidence to play the little-boy-lost role. In this way, he'll capture the heart of just the woman he needs: strong and capable, who needs just such a man as you to satisfy her maternal instincts.

The Lady Deer

You are a much more uncomplicated creature. You are a normal, well-balanced woman full of feminine charm, feminine tastes, a creature of pastel colours, delicate aspirations and a liking for the conventional manly male who is also a gentleman.

Love and Sex

The Deer people are rarely aggressive in their demands, but you remain sensual people with persistent desires. You see marriage as a union between friends, a love affair as a particularly intimate way of shaking hands and saying how-de-do.

SERPENT 27

Origins

Twenty-seventh of the 28 Chinese asterisms, situated in the Southern Palace. Chinese name: *i*. Original meaning: the wings of a bird. Position: 18° in extent, starting at α Crateris.

Your Emotional Nature

Secretive, firm-willed, suspicious of strangers yet capable of devoted love to the one right person—you of the Serpent disposition have the most complicated, fascinating emotional natures from the whole Chinese menagerie!

You cannot help feeling life in an intense manner. Emotions matter to you; they're serious, compulsive qualities that must be lived through, or risen above. Everything, from your spouse to a stray remark at a party, is important; and whether or not you like it, you hold strong opinions about these things. You cannot be budged; at worst, you're an obstinate fool—and at best, a person of resolute standards who has courage, strength and stamina.

Your emotional nature is like a lake; the deeper one descends into it, the more intense the pressure becomes. Every so often, you the introspective individual must go down into your psyche to probe the murky depths, examine the sediment. You're a fiercely self-critical person in some of your emotional attitudes. The aim of this exercise, though you may not always realise it, is to improve yourself, turn over a new leaf, rise above your baser nature. You can be a terrible taskmaster of your own psyche.

You're moody, too—especially when you're on the brink of one of your occasional upside-down turnabouts, when overnight you change your mind about a person, an object, an idea that previously you'd cherished.

You have few close friends, and even the close ones are never allowed into the precious inner recesses of your heart. But the friends you have are friends for life. You would never have chosen them in the first place if they seemed likely ever to let you down.

The Male Serpent

You have highly contradictory attitudes towards women. In some ways you view them as possessions, at other times as enemies, occasionally as equals, usually as baffling enigmas trying your patience, delighting your senses, engaging your full attention.

You're attracted first of all, towards the precious butterfly type, but they're all wrong for you. If you're to have a real ring-a-ding Serpent love match, you must pick a woman who can stand up to you, allure you from your moods, challenge your obstinacies and teach you to laugh at yourself.

The Lady Serpent

You can be a femme fatale, a vamp, a near-suicidal neurotic, or a marvellously devoted wife and mother. Usually you're all four rolled into one.

It's essential for you to have a strong man: really strong in character, genuinely tolerant of your ups and downs, with the wisdom to make up your mind for you in a way that you'd have chosen yourself if you hadn't had a man around.

Love and Sex

You have a tremendously powerful sex drive which needs to be carefully channelled if you're to find the ecstatic fulfilment in love that you deserve. One part of you—almost the puritan side—wants to transcend sexuality; the other part of you is fascinated and thrilled by it. You can be driven by jealousy, hatred as well as tearing passion.

WORM   28

Origins

Last of the 28 Chinese asterisms, situated in the Southern Palace. Chinese name: *chen*. Original meaning: a chariot platform. Position: 17° in extent, starting at γ Corvi.

You do not live your true emotions on the surface of your life. Not that you deceive people; it's just that there's a kind of fuzzy cotton-wool wall between your inner feelings and outer behaviour, so that strong inner anger comes out as mild irritation and intense inner pleasure emerges as a weak smile.

No doubt that's an exaggeration, but it gives you the general idea. On the face of it, you seem an uncomplaining person: not expecting a great deal from life, not making very strong demands on it, affable without needing company, content with your lot but not averse to changes when they come your way.

Underneath, in your real heart of hearts, you're a good deal more imaginative, caring and passionate than this, but these stronger feelings rarely emerge. Why? Partly it's your own fear of social embarrassment or, nearer the mark, of being engulfed by emotions that you can't control. And partly it's your very attractive trait, compounded of modesty, consideration for others and a genuine admission that you may be wrong, that keeps you to the middle of the road rather than fanatically veering to one side or the other.

Every so often, the strong inner emotions burst out, much to everyone's amazement—including yourself! You're the classic quiet mouse who suddenly roars like a lion, or, more appositely, the Worm that turns.

There are two recurring faults that you should try to correct. The first is agreeing with people, whatever they say. You mean well, but it becomes boring. The other potential fault is to underrate yourself; it stems from your shyness and lack of self-confidence, and you would be much happier if you had the courage to be truer to your inner fire.

The Male Worm

Part of this lack of self-confidence expresses itself in your quiet masculinity. You don't exactly brag about your virility—or, if you do, nobody believes you. All of which is unfair. Your true nature is demure, speaking in a soft, gentle voice to people you feel at home with. The right woman for you is somebody, first and foremost, who understands your need to maintain a proper balance and equilibrium in life. Friendship with a wife is far, far more important to you than temporary physical passion. As you grow older, you become more authoritative, like a calm headmaster.

The Lady Worm

You are often the girl who never pushed hard enough . . . with the consequence that many female Worms take their time in marrying, while some never marry at all.

You need a husband who will treasure you, seek to lead the same homely lifestyle that you relish, and be a constant companion. If you make the wrong choice, you'll probably carry on in life, uncomplaining if disappointed to the grave. But a few Worms rebel—suddenly, overnight—and leave their wretched husbands.

Love and Sex

Ardour burns bright in the adolescent Wormy heart, as everyone would see if only you'd rid yourself of the protective cotton-wool. But it's true to say that the Worm emotional nature wants companionship more than passion, a fond holding of the hands instead of a sweaty embrace.

THE FIFTH PATH—Your Hour of Birth

Introduction

Now we come to the final way of looking at your personality through the Chinese astrologer's eyes. In certain ways, this is the most significant approach of the whole process. You may well feel that the section in the following pages referring to your hour of birth seems to be most true of your personality. The reason for this is that, while the earlier sections have largely dealt with your inner character and aims, and the way your very subtle private emotional disposition works, this Fifth Path is concerned entirely with your outer temperament, the part of your personality that you inhabit in your daily life.

The same animals in the same order are used in Chinese astrology to correspond with the Hours as were used in the First Path to correspond with the Years. And, very largely, the same characteristics apply. The difference is that a person born in a Tiger Year will exhibit the Tiger characteristics in his overall objectives in life, while the person born during one of the Tiger two-hour stretches displays the same qualities in a much more overt superficial way.

Nobody quite knows why the Chinese associated certain times of day with particular animals. The glib answer is that every girl defending her virtue against an ungentlemanly gentleman knows perfectly well why midnight was designated the Hour of the Rat!

The obvious sensible answer is that the Chinese day began at midnight, as ours does, which is why the Rat is the first in the Chinese circle. Some people feel that the circle originated in the Middle East, and was imported into China about the third or fourth century B.C. Around the Mediterranean, the day used to begin, oddly enough, at sunset. If the Dog corresponds to the beginning of this 'day', around 8 pm, then the Rat corresponds to midnight.

The actual meanings of each animal have varied over the centuries. Once, long ago, they brought nothing but disaster. The vision of a horse in the heavens signified war; a two-headed ox meant that the temple of your ancestors would be destroyed. Worst of all, the pig brings real calamities: 'Of all the signs of evil augury, these are much the most common; they signify that a person holding public office is perverse.'

What You Have To Do

Find out from the following Table what your animal hour is. Read the characteristics given for that animal. Remember that these describe only a part of your personality: the superficial outer temperament, the skin of your psyche.

One complication is that the hours given below are based on solar time, whereas our actual clock-time can, in summer in certain countries, vary by an hour or two, due to Daylight Saving Time or so-called Summer Time.

If you know it was Summer Time, or Double Summer Time, when you were born, subtract one hour, or two hours, from your hour of birth. (In Britain, Summer Time usually extends from mid-April to early October, but was in force throughout most of the Second World War.) If you remain in doubt, and an hour's difference changes your Animal Hour, then use your commonsense to decide which animal suits your outer temperament better.

Hour	Animal	Chinese name	Meaning	
0000-0059 hrs	RAT	tzŭ	child	see page 193
0100-0259 hrs	OX	ch'ou	?	see page 194
0300-0459 hrs	TIGER	yin	reverence	see page 195
0500-0659 hrs	RABBIT	mao	bursting out	see page 196
0700-0859 hrs	DRAGON	ch'en	lucky time	see page 197
0900-1059 hrs	SNAKE	ssŭ	?	see page 198

Hour	Animal	Chinese name	Meaning	
1100-1259 hrs	HORSE	wu	south	see page 198
1300-1459 hrs	SHEEP	wei	Not yet	see page 199
1500-1659 hrs	MONKEY	shen	continuation	see page 200
1700-1859 hrs	COCK	yu	ripeness	see page 201
1900-2059 hrs	DOG	hsü	?	see page 202
2100-2259 hrs	BOAR	hai	?	see page 203
2300-2400 hrs	RAT	tzǔ	child	see page 193

THE HOUR OF THE RAT

Midnight–12.59 a.m.
11 p.m.–Midnight

Your Outer Temperament

The initial impression you make is a pleasant, amiable but sharp-eyed one. People, more often than not, will find it easy to make friends with you—or rather, to strike up an acquaintanceship, for you are more likely to have a wide circle of neighbours, colleagues at work and buddies at the local golf club or bingo parlour than many really close bosom-pals.

You strike others as a busy person, forever poking your nose into someone else's affairs simply because a mystery is an endlessly beguiling question-mark that has to be solved before you can relax. At worst a nosy-parker and gossip, at best you have a fine quest for knowledge that yearns to understand the world, Nature, the human condition and the deeper mysteries of life, death and the hereafter.

On your good days you seem brimful of snappy confidence. Sometimes this self-assurance can seem too obvious, when you appear to lay on the charm like butter. On bad days, you appear spiteful if provoked, petty over trivial matters, and somewhat insecure of your role in life. When you are really under pressure, you do not seem nearly as strong as a superficial glance seems to suggest.

THE HOUR OF THE OX

Your Outer Temperament

You seem, at first sight, to be a solid, reliable person with your head well screwed on. You appear to speak from experience, and though you may be a bit slow in making up your mind, at least you give the matter a little thought.

You strike others as a friendly, affable person, mixing easily with your own sort of people. Unfortunately, the older you get the more fixed and prejudiced you become in your social and racial attitudes, so that folk who aren't part of your 'family' strike you as odd and maybe rather undesirable.

You need to beware of this biased point of view spoiling your basically friendly ways.

You strike others as a hard-working person—not an energetic one, but a thorough, dependable individual who will stick with the job until it's finished. This certainly doesn't prevent you from relaxing, once work is over; there's nothing you love more than slouching in a favourite armchair.

At your best, you're a marvellously jovial, good-natured person. At worst, however, you've a grumpy, obstinate, rather possessive nature that is much less attractive.

Ox men and women have a lively sensuality which comes across in your daily dealings with friends and business partners and, more intimately, in your evening dates with a loved one.

THE HOUR OF THE TIGER

Your Outer Temperament

You come across in a positive, energetic and strong way that frightens timid souls but heartens most of the rest of us. A few people find you insufferable, but you accept the majority decision that you're a wonderful, wonderful person.

You usually seem self-assured (even in strange surroundings) and keen-witted. If a decision has to be made, it's you who announces the best plan of action, shouts down the opposition and goes ahead . . . and even if the consequences are a disaster, you can hopefully find somebody to blame instead of yourself.

You know, in your heart of hearts, that all this self-possession is a façade, and that underneath you may be a much more scared person than you seem. In a real crisis, the glossy image cracks, revealing a frightened individual. It's then that you wish you'd learnt to develop more humility.

All this makes you sound like Slob No. One, which is most unfair. Even when you're acting like you're the last of the big bwanas, there's still a childlike enthusiasm surrounding you that is genuinely appealing. Even when you're totally demoralised and depressed, you'll still accept the most outrageous flatteries as though they were the absolute truth.

You circulate among company with aplomb, self-esteem and charm. You seem able to fall in love with great verve —but in the last resort, even your marriage partner knows that nobody—but nobody—will ever be able to interrupt the eternal love affair between yourself and yourself.

THE HOUR OF THE RABBIT 5 am–6.59 am

Your Outer Temperament

You're a sensitive, easily roused individual with a set of vivid feelings that need to be expressed in your outer life. The only trouble is that you're also shy and fearful that you will be misunderstood by other people. So you do one of two things: either you bottle up your real emotions and express them in a fantasy life in your own imagination, or you express them disguised, dressed up, so that they're not what they seem.

In other words, you're not an easy person to grasp, at first glance; and no one should take you at face value. You don't reveal the full extent of your personality straight away, even though your heart may be bursting with desire or anger, jealousy or resentment.

It depends on your maturity whether or not you are a proper Rabbit or still a half-and-half one. The grown-up Rabbit is the one who is in control of his or her emotional nature, so that there is no fear, no anxiety—just sympathy for other people. The immature Rabbit is still controlled by his or her powerful emotional responses, and is a moody, touchy individual some times and, at others, overly affectionate.

People think they can take advantage of you, but the truth is that once you have identified with a thing, an activity, a person or an idea, you will not easily let go, and so prove tenacious in adversity.

You're enormously sentimental and gushing, given half a chance; but Rabbit men particularly are expected to put on a tougher face in the everyday world.

196

THE HOUR OF THE DRAGON

Your Outer Temperament

You seem a quizzical character at first acquaintance. With strangers you seem to have to impress them—not by your wisdom or beauty so much as your unconventionality. You need to establish that they're a bit different from other folk, that your mind works in an oddball way, that you can spot unusual similarities or suddenly pick up a stray thread and make a brilliant suggestion. Some Dragons are mad as Mad Hatters, but most of you simply seem to have this original streak in your natures that can be very appealing, or shocking, depending on how square the company is.

Nobody, including yourself, can be quite sure how you'll react, what you'll say, when you'll be bored.

You like people, but don't need their company. Although you are a very liberal-progressive person in some of your views, very conscious in your own mind of the Brotherhood of Man, you feel a bit uncomfortable in large crowds and prefer to have one friend at your side than a large mass of humanity.

You strike others as an inquisitive person always going off on your own tack. There's an independence of spirit in your psychological make-up that seems to prevent you from fitting into society as easily as most of us. Teenage Dragons can be quite perverse in the way they keep out of certain deep romantic relationships, almost as if they're frightened of being imprisoned. Their individuality is that important to them.

THE HOUR OF THE SNAKE   9 am–10.59 am

Your Outer Temperament

Your outer temperament is intense, a bit one-track and definitely strong-willed. People immediately sense that they cannot push you around, but that doesn't mean that you throw your weight about. It's more a question of seething. There's a quality of inner containment—as though you would lose your temper if you weren't so well controlled—that is noticeable in your everyday persona.

You can also be highly secretive. You aren't open by nature. Facts, particularly about your own inner feelings, have to be dragged out of you—or, more likely, coaxed out without your realising what is happening. Sometimes you present a really enigmatic face to the world, so that people simply cannot 'read' you in a straightforward way.

Obviously you don't find it easy—or desirable—to make a lot of friends. Friendship needs to be tested, if it's worth anything; mere acquaintances are all right, you think, but hardly worth the bother.

You have terrific pride—not the boastful, flaunting variety but an inner self-respect that impels you to stand firm when anyone else would give way. It's a bit of a nuisance, really.

Other people either like you or hate you—a mirror of your own nature, which tends to view life in very black-and-white terms.

THE HOUR OF THE HORSE   11 am–12.59 pm

Your Outer Temperament

The immediate impression you create is vivid, colourful· and, usually, extrovert. You pride yourself on your ability to get through to another person fast and furiously, but you don't always realise that this is a front, a façade which the other person can easily spot.

You exude a cheerful, hail-fellow-well-met image, partly because you genuinely like other people, and partly because you want to be thought a pleasant, optimistic individual.

It's a sporty, inquisitive, uncomplaining temperament. You function much better in out-of-doors, free-and-easy surroundings; grand drawing-rooms or stuffy offices don't really suit you. The popular image of the Australian—affable, unpompous, lounging around waiting for the next piece of action—may be a caricature of you . . . but a reasonably accurate one.

Your trouble is that you make a lot of noise and hullabaloo but when the cards are down and you've a real crisis on your hands, you can run away from the situation rather than stand up and fight.

People usually like you. If they don't, you may not be sensitive enough to notice, so when, months later, they explode with pent-up anger at the general way you carry on, you're totally amazed.

You carry with you an aura of happy-go-lucky good fortune that helps you out of more scrapes than you deserve.

THE HOUR OF THE SHEEP   1 pm–2.59 pm

Your Outer Temperament

You often appear sensible, undemonstrative, even a little dull—though, if there's something you want from the other person, you become a different creature: scheming, patronising, putting on an act.

People may not warm to you straight away, but you are capable of making good friends that will last a lifetime. You, in return, are not fickle; you see friendship as a question of loyalty—indeed, marriage itself is, to you, a commitment to another person that you make lovingly.

Fidelity isn't a boring duty imprisoning you; it's a gift you offer your partner.

Although you may not grab attention like more extrovert people, you gradually assume a certain amount of leadership. Instead of you creating opportunities or ambitiously pursuing your aims, you allow your natural weight and gravitas to bring you the promotion and responsibilities you are capable of carrying.

Sheep women often do not make the most of their personalities until they've a little experience under their belt. By their late twenties and thirties, they emerge as capable, attractive individuals devoted to their families and eager to play a dutiful role in local community affairs.

In the same way, Sheep men need time before the full richness of their character comes through to the surface of their personality.

HOUR OF THE MONKEY   3 pm–4.59 pm

Your Outer Temperament

You adopt a bright, clever approach to the world. You always seem tremendously alert, alive and awake; people envy you your mental energy; but in reality it's all a front. You live on the surface of your personality—and in these shallows it's easy for you to appear a big fish. If you move into deeper waters, you soon seem rather small fry.

There's a marvellously engaging appeal to your outer temperament. At your best, you seem so full of yourself, so stimulating in your ideas and conversation, so agile in your response to the surroundings in which you find yourself. You seem able to make yourself at home wherever you are; you seem able to wear the right personality to suit the people you are with.

And this is the whole trouble. Like a monkey mimicking, you go through all the right motions but don't really *mean* any of it. You say one thing while thinking another; you hold one opinion in the morning, another in the afternoon, and a third by evening; and even if you think you mean what you say, the truth is that you speak first . . . and think later.

Obviously you are adept at making friends. People usually like you, but would be fools to trust you with a secret, or rely on you in a crisis. Your great job is growing up and assuming a responsible role in the world. It can be done . . . but it's a hard task for a Monkey to master.

THE HOUR OF THE COCK 5 pm–6.59 pm

Your Outer Temperament

You appear as a hearty, self-contained person, who wants something and won't brook any interference in getting it. There's a kind of magic glamour somewhere in your personality, and if you've the verve and courage to exhibit this glamour, you can lead a very fortunate, affectionate life.

At worst, however, it turns to boastfulness, selfish tantrums and downright rudery. You have a self-centred temperament, meaning that everything that occurs to you has to be referred to *your* needs, opinions, aims and desires. Other people's requirements don't matter very much to you.

Your best qualities are your courage and confidence, the radiant personality you can project to cheer up others, your keen-witted ability to make decisions fast. You love children, sports and holidays, the fun of love affairs and the thrill of running a successful business. You hate—or are intolerant of—rainy days, dull people, failure and soberness.

You can make friends very quickly . . . or rather, you can appear friendly. Whether or not you genuinely allow them into your heart is another question. There's a pride edging into vanity that doesn't allow too much room in your affections for many people.

Crises are a real test of your moral stamina. The weak

Cock is all superficial swank, and can crumble in genuine difficulties. The mature Cock knows that proper leadership requires humility as well as the ability to give orders.

THE HOUR OF THE DOG   7 pm–8.59 pm

Your Outer Temperament

You appear to the casual observer as a dependable, steady individual who won't cause any trouble. People like you because they have nothing against you; they get on with you because there's nothing very obstreperous in your personality.

But this is a deceptive appearance. It's true that you are a loyal, persistent sort of person—true, too, that you don't go out of your way to create problems. You've a good-natured kind of temperament that appreciates a good joke, is understanding of other people's failings, and wants to play a helpful role in the community. But to call you dull is most unfair. There are positive aspects to your personality that are still valuable even if they don't clamour for attention.

The older you get, the more rounded and well-balanced you become. Most people begin as radicals and end as habit-ridden conservatives. You seem the opposite. In the early stages of your life, you seem to take things pretty much for granted; it's only after you've experienced life first-hand that it begins to dawn on you that not everything is perfect.

Don't let the rest of the world under-rate your sterling qualities. At worst you can be a bit slow and unimaginative—at best, you provide a calm presence of good sense and family togetherness.

Dog women have a lovely quiet grace of manner. Their sexuality shines through their personality without being blatant.

THE HOUR OF THE BOAR

Your Outer Temperament

You present an intelligent, slightly sardonic face to the world. The first impression you give is one of amused interest in what's going on around you. You don't seem to get tremendously involved yourself, and shy away from an overstrong response from other people—especially gushing females.

As people get to know you better—and you don't make real friends that easily—they discern a much more human, sensitive creature lurking underneath this slightly superior façade. You keep people at a distance not because you dislike them but due to a somewhat shy, embarrassed feeling when they start to get too intimate. You dislike 'soppy' feelings so much that you run the danger of not distinguishing between sentimental emotions and genuine heartfelt sentiment.

You'll gather that most acquaintances aren't quite certain what to make of you. Certainly some Boars enjoy being 'characters', playing to the gallery for all they're worth. Others among you, lacking self-confidence in personal relationships, are uncertain how you'll behave in a given situation. Although you seem self-sufficient in most ways, you benefit from quite a strong marriage partner who can counteract these doubts with a lively but solid manner.

At your best, you are stimulating company when your interest is roused. But there is a lazy streak in your nature which can spoil the edge to your personality.

THE PATHS CONVERGE

To know how all these paths combine to form your total personality, you should understand one or two basic principles.

The Hand

The number five plays a highly significant role in ancient Chinese thought. They considered that there were five elements in nature, that the sky was divided into five segments or palaces, that there were five planets, five colours, five flavours and so on.

It's obvious, too, that there are five fingers on your hand —or rather, four fingers and a thumb. The distinction is necessary, because the Chinese thought this four-plus-one-equals-five principle very important. Their division of the sky was really four palaces corresponding to north, south, east and west—and a fifth palace, centred at the pole star, around which the other four revolved.

It's the same with your fingers and thumbs. Each digit has its own characteristics, but one of them—the thumb—stands out from the rest and provides, in a sense, the will-power and energy to get the others working. It's common knowledge, for instance, that a new-born baby with a powerfully splayed thumb will soon have a mind of its own.

Think of the hand symbolising your personality, and the five digits corresponding with the Fivefold Path of Year, Season, Fortnight, Day and Hour. One path will correspond with the thumb, one with the index finger, and so forth down to the little finger.

To decide which path correlates with which digit, you have to determine whether you're a *yin* or a *yang* person.

Yin and Yang

These words are fairly commonly used nowadays, so you probably know that the Chinese saw a dualistic principle at work throughout life: male and female, positive and negative, hot and cold, dry and wet, heaven and earth right down to day and night. *Yang* was male; *yin* was female.

There's no foolproof way of saying which one you are. Certainly you shouldn't jump to the conclusion that because you're a man you're *yang*, or a woman you're *yin*. Besides, it's highly unlikely—and undesirable—that any of us should be all *yang* and no *yin*, or the other way round.

To help you make a subjective judgment about your *yin-yang* balance, answer the following questions and tot up the scores at the end: —

If you were brave enough, which of these sports would you tackle?
  A Mountaineering
  B Football
  C Underwater diving

When you pick up a magazine, how do you read it?
  A From front to back
  B Here and there
  C Back to front

Which colour do you identify with?
  A Red
  B Yellow
  C Blue

In music, which sound thrills you the most?
  A Trumpet solo
  B Drums
  C Violins

What is your favourite way of spending an evening?
   A   Going somewhere new
   B   Going somewhere familiar
   C   Staying comfortably at home

When is your best time of day?
   A   Mornings
   B   Afternoons
   C   Evenings

Which shape seems to symbolise your character best?
   A   Arrow
   B   Square
   C   Circle

As you may have guessed by now, the A answers correspond with *yang* and the C answers with *yin*. If A or C received the greater score, then you can see whether you're *yin*-or *yang*-inclined. (If the scores are equal, go to the questions you marked B and force yourself to decide on A or C.)

You may feel that this test is unfair or too trivial. If so, go back to the general principles behind *yin* and *yang* and decide on your own account which your character suits.

The *yin* person is sympathetic to others, wanting to listen to their problems and share their joys and sorrows. If you're largely *yin*, you might see yourself as a mirror, a bowl or concave person who receives more from the world than you give. In other words, the important experiences in your life mark big changes in your own feelings and attitudes.

The *yang* person, on the other hand, is more outward-looking, forceful and active. As a largely *yang* person, you would want to achieve a lot in life, and you would want to leave your impression on the people around you. You would see yourself as a pioneer of new ideas; you would be interested in the future more than the past; and you might be a little self-centred, even though—unlike the *yin* folk—you would seek to give more to the world than you receive.

Left and Right

Now that you've decided, more or less, which principle your character seems to adhere to, let's go back to the hand. Remember the order of the Fivefold Path: Year, Season, Fortnight, Day and Hour. If you look at your left hand, palm upward, with the thumb on the left, you see the arrangement of the Path for the *yin* people. In their case, it is the Year which is represented by the odd man out, the thumb, the Season which is symbolised by the index finger and, at the other end, the Hour which corresponds with the little finger.

The *yin* person, which is the feminine principle in life, is going to get a sense of direction from that part of her personality called the Season, because it's the index finger that points, wags, gives instructions and generally communicates ideas and feelings. But her real inner strength —the kind of person she is at rock bottom, so to speak— will come from that part of her character called the Year, for it is the thumb which presses when real force must be exerted and which is used as an identification-mark in place of the signature. So what about the little finger? It is used for balance, when delicacy is required to counteract the brute strength of the thumb. So the *yin* person uses that part of her psyche called the Hour as a subtle grace-note to add poise and decorum.

For the *yang* person, the reverse is true. The right hand held palm upward has the thumb on the right and the little finger on the left. His strength and stamina comes from the Hour part of his character, his direction in life from the Day, and the subtleties of his surface behaviour from the Year.

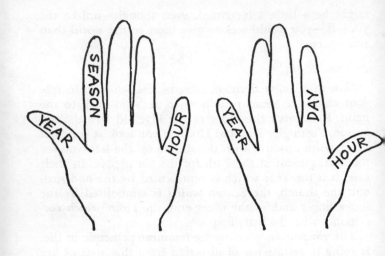

LEFT HAND = yin　　　**RIGHT HAND = yang**

Examples

John and Yoko Ono Lennon

John was born on 9th October 1940, at approximately 5 a.m. GMT. So his Year is DRAGON. He wants power, but will only use subtle, original ways to obtain it—with the results that his efforts can sometimes be self-defeating. The alert mind, the witty conversation, the desire for independence—all are clearly present in John's whole basic approach to life.

At a spiritual level, his season is METAL. In his ideal moments, he'll wish to express truth, art and culture in his everyday life, and seek to lead a sensitive, gentle life-style.

His fortnight is No 17 COLD DEWS, corresponding to the sign of Libra. Here is his career orientation towards the arts, both music and writing. Here, too, an interesting demonstration of the way he cannot, for all his Dragon independence, actually work a great deal on his own; he needs the collaboration, first of the other Beatles, then of his wife Yoko.

His animal Asterism is No 7, the LEOPARD. Here is the vain, theatrical emotional disposition that drew him to pop music in the first place; the slightly laconic, drawling way he has in talking; and the undoubted appeal, not simply sexual, that he has for many people throughout the world.

Finally, his Animal Hour is either TIGER or RABBIT, depending on whether he was born just before 5 a.m. or just after. Frankly I prefer the 'correct' Rabbit, to account for the relatively subdued, sensitive outer temperament hiding the more boastful Leopard inside. If John had a Tiger outer facade, he would be much more extrovert and pushy than he really is.

Yoko was born on 18th February 1933 at 8.20 p.m. So her Year is COCK. Anyone who has met her realises that beneath her relatively quiet, demure outer personality (see below) there's a formidable will-power, a strong competitiveness, and the love of adventure associated with Cock people. With Yoko the pioneering spirit emerges as a delight in the bizarre.

Her season is WATER—at her best, she does exude a comforting, motherly image, and her concern for her child is apparent to all.

Her fortnight is No 1 BEGINNING OF SPRING. Her career has touched many areas, but throughout her work she's been concerned with a rational, reasonable, truthful understanding of nature, including human nature. It is through her humanitarian impact that John has become interested in social and political matters. She is clearly a revolutionary in these fields.

Her emotional disposition is established by her Animal Asterism, which is No 23 SHEEP. This combination of the tender and materialistic, common-sensical and psychic, absolutely gets to the heart of the way Yoko responds to the life around her.

Finally, her Animal Hour is DOG. Like John, this relatively undemonstrative façade hides the inner strength and originality.

They make a good combination. The Dragon in him responds to the Cock in her; as it says, Yoko may sometimes seem too dominant to John, and he too tricky and devious to her—but it's an enterprising, never-dull relationship.

Teddy Kennedy was born on 22nd February 1932 at 3.58 am. His year, appropriately enough, is MONKEY. He is the quintessential politician, persuading, orating, button-holing colleagues, trying his hand at a wide variety of tasks. Every politician needs to be flexible, which Teddy clearly is.

His season is WATER, meaning that his spiritual aspirations concern the comfort and emotional ease of the world.

His fortnight is No 2 RAIN, corresponding to the beginning of Pisces. Clearly Teddy, like all the Kennedys, is motivated by idealism, the Just Cause, and sympathy for others.

His Animal Asterism is No 17 PHEASANT. Teddy's love of the good life, his ability to be on good acquaintance with everyone, and his tendency to be a bit pompous on occasion all point to the appositeness of his Pheasant emotional disposition.

His Animal Hour is TIGER. Read the characteristics of this animal—strong, self-assured, vain—to see the kind of impact this magnetic public figure arouses in others. But bearing in mind that fatal car crash in 1969, note one sentence in the Tiger section: 'In a real crisis, the glossy image cracks; revealing a frightened individual. It's then that you wish you'd learnt to develop more humility.'

Queen Elizabeth II was born on April 21st 1926 at 1.40 am. Her Animal Year is TIGER, as befits a monarch who rules over many millions of British subjects. Her Season, WOOD, tells a similar story for a constitutional queen; for the Wood ideal is to become the civilised member of society.

Her fortnight is No 6 GRAIN RAIN. Nobody doubts that the Queen tackles her work with great dependability. As it says, 'fast-talking, quick-thinking situations don't suit', and Her Majesty, as a natural conservative, clearly holds a position of trust and respectability in society.

Her Animal Asterism is No 7 LEOPARD. Like John Lennon she is in a branch of show-business, whether she likes it or not; both of them have this capacity to radiate an inner magnetism in public; and, maybe, the Queen, too, is a little vain. Certainly she doesn't seem to object to the trappings of splendour with which she's surrounded.

Her Animal Hour is OX. Again this combination of solid reliability coupled with affability seems absolutely correct.

THE PATH AHEAD

We have seen how the Five Paths become the five fingers of the hand. When the Paths converge, the fingertips are brought together so that the hand, symbol of Man's psyche, resembles a lotus-flower, or water-lily, in bud. This bud is your soul at birth, innocent of experience yet containing all the promise of the fully-opened blossom.

In the course of your lifetime, the flower blooms, the fingers open, the Five Paths seek expression in the various departments of life: career, home and family, love with the proper partner. The lotus, symbol of Man's perfect life on earth, is peaceful. It floats on the waters, as all of us are borne on the Water of Life. No one petal strives for dominance; all open and close, in obedience to the Divine Light above, until life is spent, the flower wilts, and the plant is swallowed up by the waters beneath.

In just the same way, each human soul enters this world from the waters of the womb. Each of us, to the best of our ability, must unfold our petals in harmony, giving due attention to the needs of the spirit as much as to the body, to the mind as much as to the desires. Throughout our life, we are sustained by the Light and Water, the father and mother of the Godhead. And at our death, we seem to disappear—until another season, another waxing of the light.

In ancient China, the astrologers watched the progress of Jupiter to predict plenty or scarcity, peace or war, according to the planet's colour, brilliance and position in the heavens. In the same way, we can detect when the beneficent influence of Jupiter will bring extra sunshine, so to speak, to our lotus petals, when our Five Paths will seem easy, and we bask in happiness, success and well-being. The following Table tells you when, according to your Fortnight and Animal Asterism, you will receive an additional blessing in the years ahead.

Fortnight Number	Dates when you can reasonably expect some good news to do with your career, when your affairs will appear successful and when a certain amount of luck seems to be coming your way.
1 Beginning of Spring	January—March 1974 June—August 1977
2 Rain	March—May 1974 September—December 1977 April—June 1978
3 Waking Up	June—August 1974 January—March 1975 July—August 1978
4 Spring	March—May 1975 September 1978—July 1979
5 Clear & Bright	June 1975—March 1976
6 Grain Rain ·	April—May 1976 October 1979—August 1980
7 Summer	June—August 1976 November 1976—March 1977
8 Lesser Fullness	March—December 1973 September—October 1976 April—June 1977 November—December 1980
9 Grain in Ear	see 1 above
10 Summer Solstice	see 2 above
11 Lesser Heat	see 3 above
12 Greater Heat	see 4 above
13 Autumn	see 5 above
14 End of Heat	see 6 above
15 White Dews	see 7 above
16 Autumn Equinox	see 8 above
17 Cold Dews	see 1 above

18	Descent of Hoar Frost	see 2 above
19	Beginning of Winter	see 3 above
20	Lesser Snow	see 4 above
21	Greater Snow	see 5 above
22	Winter Solstice	see 6 above
23	Lesser Cold	see 7 above
24	Greater Cold	see 8 above

Animal Asterism	Dates when you can reasonably expect some emotional uplift, a feeling that you're riding a crest of a wave. An extravagant, generous, happy-go-lucky time, broadly speaking.
1 Hornless Dragon	January—February 1974 June—July 1977
2 Dragon	March 1974—April 1974 August 1977—January 1978 April—June 1978
3 Badger	May 1974—February 1975 June—July 1978
4 Hare	March—April 1975 August—October 1978
5 Fox	April—June 1975 October 1978—January 1979 June—July 1979
6 Tiger	February—March 1976 August—September 1979
7 Leopard	April—May 1976 October—December 1979
8 Gryphon	June—July 1976
9 Ox	February—April 1973 August—November 1976 March—May 1977

10	Bat	May—July 1973
		December 1973—January 1974
		June—July 1977
11	Rat	February—March 1974
		July 1977—May 1978
12	Swallow	April 1974—January 1975
		May—August 1978
13	Boar	February—March 1975
		July—September 1978
		February—May 1979
14	Porcupine	April—May 1975
		October 1978—January 1979
		May—July 1979
15	Wolf	May 1975—March 1976
		July—September 1979
16	Dog	March—May 1976
		September—December 1979
17	Pheasant	May—July 1976
		December 1976—February 1977
18	Cock	February—March 1973
		July—December 1976
		March—April 1977
19	Raven	April—July 1973
		November 1973—January 1974
		May—June 1977
20	Monkey	January—March 1974
		July—August 1977
21	Ape	March—May 1974
		September—December 1974
		September—December 1977
		May—June 1978
22	Tapir	June—August 1974
		January—March 1975
		June—August 1978
23	Sheep	March—April 1975
		August 1978—June 1979

24	Muntjak	May—July 1975
		September 1975—February 1976
		July—August 1979
25	Horse	July—August 1975
		March—April 1976
		September—October 1979
26	Deer	April—June 1976
		November—December 1979
27	Serpent	January—March 1973
		June 1976—April 1977
28	Worm	March—December 1973
		April—June 1977

A FAREWELL TALE

Confucius went to see Lao Tan, who said to him: 'I hear you are a wise man from the North. Have you yet found the Path?'

'Not yet,' replied Confucius.

'How did you begin to search for it?' said Lao Tan.

'I sought it in measures and numbers,' answered Confucius, 'but after five years I still had not found it.'

'And how then did you seek it?'

'I sought it in the Yin and the Yang, but after twelve more years I still did not find it.'

'Just so,' said Lao Tan. 'If the Path could be offered from person to person, all men would present it to their rulers. If it could be served up in bowls, all men would have given it to their parents. If it could be talked about, everyone would have told their brothers. If it could be inherited, men would have left it to their sons and grandsons.

'But no-one could do any of these things. Because if you have not already got it within your heart, you cannot receive it.'

To Angelina

Wishing you all the best.

From A Special Friend to a
Special Friend

FRIENDSHIP
REMAINS
AND
NEVER
CAN
END